Ask the Mule Deer Guides

Ask the Mule Deer Guides

by

J. Y. Jones

SAFARI PRESS INC.

The trademark Safari Press ® is registered with the U.S. Patent and Trademark Office and in other countries.

Jones, J. Y

First edition

Safari Press

2009, Long Beach, California

ISBN 1-57157-325-9

Library of Congress Catalog Card Number: 2007941588

10 9 8 7 6 5 4 3 2 1

Printed in China

Readers wishing to receive the Safari Press catalog, featuring many fine books on big-game hunting, wingshooting, and sporting firearms, should write to Safari Press Inc., P.O. Box 3095, Long Beach, CA 90803, USA. Tel: (714) 894-9080, or visit our Web site at www.safaripress.com.

DEDICATION

It's always a pleasure to decide to whom or to what to dedicate a book, because that's usually among the final steps in turning the book over to the publisher and "putting it to bed." So I naturally have pondered the question, but it really isn't hard to come up with the right answer because wisdom and truth don't change with my personal whims. This dedication will echo many of the sentiments I've expressed in my other books.

Ask the Mule Deer Guides is rightly dedicated to the hard-working guides who are featured in its pages, plus myriad others who, for various reasons, could not be included. The guides in this book are representative of the very best in the mule deer hunting fraternity, but inevitably I could not include many others equally qualified, to whom I also dedicate this book. If you are an ethical, law-abiding mule deer guide, you can consider yourself one of the recipients of this honor.

I must also include those decent and good hunters who follow those guides, as well as the self-guided mule deer hunter, in whatever state or province. It is the interest and input of such individuals that have resulted in a resurgence of mule deer populations across much of the mule deer's native range. For lack of such grass-roots enthusiasm, any government program is bound to fail.

It is prudent also to include the state game agencies responsible for managing our magnificent mule deer resource, and I would particularly single out Colorado for its bold step of putting mule deer on a draw basis statewide, flying in the face of history and tradition to do something important for the good of the animal. In high-quality habitat, all it takes to have excellent mule deer hunting and high-quality trophies is good management with a limited harvest on a reasonable quota. Colorado has demonstrated how well that works. As an aside, I would call on them, and all other states that manage mule deer for quality, to continue this program and not be tempted to issue more tags than scientific management dictates.

There are some private organizations that promote mule deer management, among them the Mule Deer Foundation, and

I include them in this dedication. Also, I dedicate this book to the many hunting publications and organizations that promote sound administration of mule deer populations, such as *Muley Crazy* and *The Huntin' Fool,* Safari Club International, the North American Hunting Club, and the National Rifle Association.

Finally, as always, I must dedicate this minuscule work to the Creator of the great North American West and all it contains, as well as everything else our senses can perceive. This infinite God also assembled out of nothing the magnificent mule deer, and placed in the heart of every hunter a passion for seeing and seeking such great beasts of the field. His creating agent, according to the Bible, is His holy Son, Jesus Christ, God incarnate, who came in the flesh, lived a perfect life, died a terrible death on a cruel cross on my behalf, and rose again to eternal life that I might live forever with Him. As the Gospel of John states so eloquently, No one has seen God at any time; the only begotten God, who is in the bosom of the Father, He has explained Him. In Christ we have the only complete revelation of God, because Christ is the full explanation of God. For those who can accept this, they receive true spiritual vision, and that by His grace alone.

TABLE OF CONTENTS

FOREWORD

I've got to admit it. I dreaded reading this book. I procrastinated, found excuses, but I'd promised J.Y. and my publisher I'd write a foreword, and a promise is a promise.

I was pleasantly surprised.

Not to brag, honest, but I started hunting mule deer the best part of four decades ago in Mexico's Sonoran Desert as a kid when the Model '94 I toted weighed as much as I did. Sarge Brown and I'd simply ride horses across the two-strand, barbed-wire border fence, ask a ranchero to hunt, and bribe the border guards on both sides with bootleg mescal and venison on the way back.

Since that time, I've bagged 70 trophy bucks over 4½ years old (200 mule deer total) in most of the Western states and two Canadian provinces. I've spent a dozen years as a wildlife biologist studying their mortality, ecology, and behavior, and I've written three books on mule deer and mule deer hunting (get my latest, *Mule Deer Quest,* from Safari Press). I've made fifty or so hunts overseas, mostly in Asia and Africa, and four times that in North America, and I'm convinced that the guy who consistently bags good mule deer bucks is the best nimrod on the planet. With the exception of three hunts in two Canadian provinces, I haven't used a mule deer guide. But guides are guides, and I've hired at least a hundred of them on four continents, so I know a good one.

Meet the Mule Deer Guides is a must-read for the first-time mule deer hunter and for that matter, anyone contemplating his first guided mule deer hunt. Guides are individuals and often own different and strong opinions on a variety of subjects. Perhaps the important part of this book is not so much the dogma of a given guide, but the exposure for the new mule deer hunter to a variety of ideas.

Guide opinions differ, and I don't agree with all of their views, either, but it's nice to find many that support what decades in mule deer country have taught me. When prospecting for a guide, I'd agree with Grant Adkisson, ". . . ask for references from hunters who were not successful." Doug Gardner is right, too, ". . . I tell them they have two chances [at a B&B buck]—slim and none." Thomas Brunson looks for honesty, and Troy Justensen says, ". . . experience over anything else."

Some guides place undue importance on preseason scouting. From my four decades watching mule deer, I know that adult bucks may change home ranges as many as six times in a year. I often locate good bucks down the hill while I'm driving to my campus office during the summer, but I can bet a paycheck they'll disappear before the opener, and they do. Scouting works if it's close to the opener and the buck doesn't sense you. Look for big buck "sign," then get out until the hunt. I agree with David Lopez, who looks for tracks.

I'd like to hunt with top Mexican guide David Lopez. Our philosophies parallel. He notes mule deer are getting scarce, he likes patient hunters that are ". . . a good walker..." (though many guides in this tome claim walking isn't important), and believes good boots are the most important hunter gear. Thankfully, most guides here play down gadget importance like a GPS (Robb Wiley and Harry Leuenberger), and most rate the binocular the most important gear. To me, it's a good boot and a good binoc, in that order.

In locating big bucks, Jeff Chadd reflects my philosophy: ". . . stay off the beaten path . . . find those pockets where nobody else goes." Four out of five of my trophy bucks came from precisely such places. Thomas Brunson says to look for, among other things, water when locating bucks, but water is less important for mule deer than it is for even desert bighorn sheep; mule deer go six months without free water in the desert because they get moisture from vegetation. I like Nick Frederick's ". . . measuring tapes have ruined more hunts. . . ."

The best advice in the book, though, comes from Lopez again: "Never give up."

Walt Prothero
Buck Creek, Utah
March 2008

INTRODUCTION AND ACKNOWLEDGMENTS

As with all other books in this series, many fine people have contributed to the project. Before I try my best to name them all, I want to give an overview of the book. Mule deer are the favorite game of many hunters in North America, and those who guide hunters successfully to good bucks year after year have been given a forum here to express themselves. Perhaps that is the most significant aspect of *Ask the Mule Deer Guides.*

The basic layout of this book is similar to that of the preceding ones in the series *(Ask the Elk Guides, Ask the Whitetail Guides, and Ask the Black Bear Guides).* Each guide had to be recommended by someone on my big list of contacts in the hunting community, and then had to show me enough experience and success that I felt he qualified. Also, I had to be assured, inasmuch as is possible, that each guide operates with the highest integrity. Once those hurdles had been passed, I sent the selected guides the list of questions, and in most cases a final interview was conducted by telephone.

The format of this book returns to the regional concept, rather than the hunting-method approach used in *Ask the Black Bear Guides.* The questions are little changed from the previous books, though I have tried to make this volume somewhat more interesting to hunters who want to garner information on self-guided hunting of mule deer.

As usual, I can't thank the participating guides enough. It's my hope that the effort and cooperation they have put forth will lead to good things for them in the future. My thanks also to all who have suggested guides, whether I used them in the book or not. I would point out for special recognition Brent Sinclair, one of North America's top guides himself and one included as a featured guide in *Ask the Elk Guides.* He has been of immense help with all of my books, and he suggested two of the guides in this series. He has also submitted his own set of mule deer photos for use in this book.

Jack Atcheson, Jr., has also been incredibly valuable in assembling all of the books so far completed in this series, and at least one guide he's recommended has made it into each of the first four books. Others who suggested guides included Brian Latturner of MonsterMuleys.com, Gary Tennison, my publisher Ludo Wurfbain, John Green, Richard Stockmar, Alberto de Jongh, Robert Taylor, Eric Albus, Ron Spomer, Craig Kauffman, Mike Simpson, Herb Atkinson, Raymond Yu, Rex Baker Jr., and Glen Coolahan. I could not include all of the guides suggested, but I hope I've chosen some of the best.

Finally, I want to thank my wife for letting me spend hours on the telephone and at the computer to get this one done. Her patience is legendary, and I love her dearly.

Chapter 1

MEET THE MULE DEER GUIDES

It is with great pleasure that I introduce mule deer hunters everywhere to perhaps the best assemblage of mule deer guides ever featured in one piece of literature.* From the youngest to the oldest, these guides are the most experienced group imaginable, and each has guided for an average of more than twenty-five years. All are still actively outfitting and guiding. They have a cumulative experience of over three hundred years of guiding for mule deer. All have a wealth of information to share, and what they have to say may open your eyes to a whole new world with respect to guide-client relations. I believe that anyone who has ever been guided on a mule deer hunt will find himself described somewhere in the pages of this book.

These guides share a large number of characteristics in common. They universally place a high premium on hunter ethics, honesty, integrity, hard work, patience, dependability, and persistence. They all desire their hunters to come well prepared in every possible way, and they go into great detail delineating how one goes about doing this. Despite the commonality of such thoughts, their individual words are unique and different, so the reader never gets bored.

These guides are truly excellent representatives of the outdoor fraternity, and I think you'll agree they all offer invaluable insights into the world of mule deer hunting. I can't think of a sufficient way to repay them for imparting their wealth of experience to us, the mule deer hunters of today, so thank them yourself when you see them . . . and enjoy the information here to the utmost!

*Each guide can be found here in the sequence they appear in the book, with a brief summary of their backgrounds and experience, contact information, and a recent photograph. The material included here is taken directly from interviews with the guides and some cases from printed material they supplied. Most information in this book has been obtained by means of telephone interviews with each guide, and is essentially as they said it.

Ask the Mule Deer Guides

Grant Adkisson
Adkisson Outdoors
P.O. Box 39
Canyon City, CO 81215
719-275-7777
grantadkisson@earthlink.net

Grant Adkisson began guiding on his family's ranch in 1963 when he was only thirteen years old, and he's been at it ever since, chalking up forty-four years of active guiding. Both sides of Grant's family were homesteaders in Colorado. One grandfather raised cattle for gold miners in the 1800s and later outfitted for Teddy Roosevelt. So far Grant has guided more than a thousand hunters on big-game hunts.

Grant is an avid bow hunter who took his first buck with a bow when he was thirteen. He has taken every species of big-game animal in Colorado with a longbow, and was inducted into the Colorado Hunting Hall of Fame for that feat. One of his biggest joys is in helping others appreciate the creation and introducing them to the Creator in the process.

He keeps an extremely busy schedule apart from his guiding activities. He also writes some magazine articles, most with a slant that meshes well with his personal ministry and philosophy. He is a life member of numerous hunting and conservation organizations, including Pope and Young, Boone and Crockett, Safari Club International, and the Rocky Mountain Elk Foundation.

He's a fan of publications put out by those groups, and he also collects outdoor books, with more than six thousand in his personal library, many of them old and many first editions. A lot of his new books come from Safari Press because he loves the books that company publishes. He likes to read *Sports Afield*, which he believes is now one of the top outdoor publications in the industry.

Jeff Chadd
Majestic Mountain Lakeview
Outfitters
P.O. Box 1000
Lake City, CO 81235
970-944-2263
sheephunter@lakecity.net
www.mmlo.net

   Jeff has been living and guiding in Alaska for sheep and other animals for most of the past twenty-five years, and he is an Alaska master guide. He met an outfitter from Colorado at a sports show some years ago, and the two hit it off. That individual convinced Jeff to come down to Colorado and guide for him after finishing his sheep hunts in Alaska, and the arrangement worked out very well. Four years ago Jeff moved to Colorado with his family, and he's fallen in love with his new home. He's been guiding for seventeen years for mule deer in Colorado and Montana and shows no sign of slowing down. He's personally guided at least eighty to a hundred hunters for mule deer, and probably more. For all species, he believes he's guided almost a thousand hunters in his career. He does it for the simple reason that he loves the outdoors and the challenge of the hunt. One of his favorite publications is Ryan Hatch's magazine *Muley Crazy,* which is based in Utah.

Ask the Mule Deer Guides

Robb Wiley
Non-Typical Outfitters
P.O. Box 3644
Alpine, WY 83128
wiley@silverstar.com
www.non-typical-outfitters.com

Robb began guiding for mule deer in 1992, but prior to that he had laid a firm foundation with a basic passion for hunting mule deer. When he decided to go into guiding more intensively, he figured that the best way to learn how to do it was to work for the best of the best, so he sought them out and worked for several high-quality outfitters. After those experiences, he began thinking of moving to some superlative place to chase real trophy mule deer, and that led him to western Wyoming, where he lives today. He now guides for trophy mule deer, as well as for elk and black bear. He has personally guided some two hundred mule deer hunters over the years, and readily confesses that big mule deer are his passion. He spends a tremendous amount of time year-round on one aspect or another of mule deer hunting: He observes mule deer on their wintering grounds, hunts sheds in the spring, and begins scouting bucks when they are in the velvet in summer. He points to the thrill of helping others through a hunt, hunters who might not have the experience and skills to do it on their own. He loves that aspect of his work because it adds another element of challenge to getting a big buck. For reading materials, Robb relates that *Muley Challenge*, *Eastman's Journal,* and *Sports Afield* are his favorites.

Keith Atcheson
Jack Atcheson & Sons, Inc.
Hunters Montana
3210 Ottawa
Butte, MT 59701
406-782-2382
keith@atcheson.com
www.atcheson.com

Keith began guiding elk and mule deer hunters in his home state of Montana in 1976 at the age of sixteen. He grew up in the family business of Jack Atcheson & Sons, Inc. and Atcheson Taxidermy, so he was exposed to hunting from a very young age. He remembers his first client, a doctor from Nevada: They were hunting in the rugged Madison Range in two or three feet of snow and twenty-below zero temperatures. The client passed up several excellent mule deer bucks in his desire for a really big bull elk. It's a long story, but the client never did get his big bull, and the experience was perhaps the most negative of Keith's career.

Despite that rough first experience he still actively guides. Over the last thirty-one years, Keith's outfitting business has had well over a thousand clients, and he has personally guided some five hundred hunters. He continues to guide because he enjoys it, and in particular he likes to introduce new hunters to the sport. He feels it is very important to teach hunters how to conduct themselves safely and effectively in the field, as well as to respect the animals they hunt. He advocates using traditional methods and making hunting a way of life.

His favorite hunting magazines are *Sports Afield, American Hunter,* and *Grey's Sporting Journal.* Keith also likes classic books written by famous writers and professional hunters such as Jack O'Connor, Craig Boddington, Ron Spomer, Bull Baertle, and Robert Ruark.

Ask the Mule Deer Guides

Doug Gardner
Powder River Outfitters
P.O. Box 257
2770 Hammond Road
Hammond, MT 59332
406-427-5721
dkg-hunters@hotmail.com
www.powder-river-outfitters.com

Doug started guiding in the mid-1970s on his ranch in eastern Montana. His family had always welcomed hunters, but they began guiding them professionally only in 1976. When he got the opportunity to manage a neighbor's ranch, which was the largest in Montana, he took the chance. Their first years were lean. Then Doug got a really good break when he met an outfitter, his soon-to-be partner, who had hunters but no good place to hunt. Their handshake was the beginning of Powder River Outfitters, more than thirty years ago.

Doug still guides actively and has taken more than two thousand hunters afield for all species, but predominantly mule deer. He has enjoyed meeting some great people over the years and has made some lifelong friends; he views it as a wonderful addition to his own ranch to host hunters.

Doug takes *North American Hunter* and *Petersen's Hunting,* and he used to read Jack O'Connor's classic material in *Outdoor Life.* He's read some of Theodore Roosevelt's books, particularly those dealing with his own area of Montana; in fact, Doug states that Roosevelt hunted buffalo right there on their ranch.

Doug and his wife have three children. Their oldest son is a petroleum engineer and a dedicated hunter who sometimes guides for them. They also have a daughter who is going to medical school, and their youngest son is still in high school but looks like he's going to be their upcoming rancher and outfitter.

Fred Lamphere
Dakota Ranch Outfitters
P.O. Box 342
Newell, SD 57760
605-456-2974
bcso1@rushmore.com
www.dakotaranchoutfitters.com

Fred started guiding when he was about fourteen years old, primarily helping people who didn't know their way around his uncle's ranch. Back in those days he wasn't an experienced hunter, but he knew the ranch. He was a natural hunter from an early age, though, and was usually able to get people where they needed to be. Those beginnings were almost thirty years ago, and he's been guiding ever since, with no plans to stop doing so anytime in the foreseeable future. He's guided about four hundred hunters personally, and does so mostly because he likes to build appreciation for the beautiful area in which he lives. Fred is not only a guide and outfitter but also the sheriff of Butte County, South Dakota (though he also conducts hunts in adjacent Wyoming and Montana). He enjoys target magazines such as *Big Buck* and *Trophy Hunter,* publications that are specific to the area he hunts and the type of game available there.

Ask the Mule Deer Guides

Thomas and Jamie Brunson
HC 33 Box 33123
Ely, NV 89318
775-289-3311
timberlineguide@sbcglobal.net
www.timberlineoutfittersnevada.com

Thomas is one of the newer guides in this book, having begun his career in 2000. At that time he was playing college baseball and looking for direction, and he had received several offers to continue his athletic career. He'd been hunting all his life and genuinely felt that such a vocation was his calling. At the urging of his parents he began doing what he really loved, and according to Thomas it's been working out very well. He's in the guiding and outfitting business full time now, mainly in Nevada, and he does taxidermy in the summer when he's not guiding.

He was only twenty when he started his business, and he anticipates actively guiding for many years. He has personally guided about one hundred hunters, mainly for mule deer and elk. His wife, Jamie, is an integral part of the business and is involved in every aspect, except the actual guiding. Thomas's reasons for guiding involve his love for the mountains and his passion for hunting.

According to Thomas, they subscribe to every hunting magazine in existence! *Muley Crazy* is probably his favorite, but he also likes *Trophy Hunter, Eastman's Journal,* and *Hunters Illustrated.* He really enjoyed David Long's new book *Public Land Muleys,* which he just finished. He has also read, liked, and would recommend Cameron Haines's *High Country Muleys.*

Troy Justensen
X-Treme Outfitters
P.O. Box 133
Kaysville, UT 84037
801-557-3362
xtremeoutfitter@aol.com
www.xtremeoutfitting.com

Troy began his career in guiding in 1992. He had always had a passion for hunting, and at that time he worked for a gentleman in the construction industry. His employer had drawn a limited-entry mule deer permit and wanted to get the biggest mule deer he could with that precious tag. He started sending Troy down into the area where he had drawn to do some looking, giving him leave from the construction site, and that got the ball rolling. Later Troy signed on to guide at the Heaton Ranch, a big spread in the Paunsaugunt region of Utah that takes quite a few hunters each year. Not too long afterward Troy started his own guiding business, and he isn't expecting to stop guiding anytime soon.

He has personally guided some 150 hunters for mule deer, plus many more for other species. He guides simply because he loves it. He says that there are a lot of terrific hunts in Utah where he has low odds of ever drawing a tag, and that a lot of hunts are so expensive he may never get to go on one himself. However, as a guide he gets to experience everything except pulling the trigger.

He highly recommends *Muley Crazy* as the best of all the publications. Troy is also serious about sheep hunting and enjoys *Wild Sheep,* published by the Foundation for North American Wild Sheep. He also reads Garth Carter's publication *The Huntin' Fool.*

Ask the Mule Deer Guides

Jess Rankin
West Tex–New Mex Hunting
Services
P.O. Box 2305
Roswell, NM 88202
505-622-6600
letshunt@zianet.com
www.new-mexico-hunts.com

Jess had never actually guided for a living until 1986. He had been out of college for several years and was working in agricultural sales, and from that experience he developed a good relationship with a lot of ranchers in his part of the country. Jess loved to hunt, so he decided to start an outfitting business, now known to many hunters as West Tex–New Mex Hunting Services.

He still sometimes guides hunters personally, but during the busiest times he's too involved with running several camps to get into the field with hunters. He notes that there are always problems that the camp manager can't handle, and guiding can distract him from oversight of the operation. Whenever possible, though, he still likes to get out into the field. Jess has personally guided about two hundred hunters. He likes being in business for himself and particularly enjoys his current line of work.

Jess was born on a ranch in west Texas, and thus he gets along well with ranchers and ranching people. Also, he relates well to hunters in general and to many different types of people. He says that he doesn't read nearly as much as he once did, due to the pressures of running a business, but that he has always liked *Petersen's Hunting*. He believes Garth Carter's newsletter, *The Huntin' Fool,* to be one of the best pieces of hunting literature around. He also likes *Trophy Hunter* and *Eastman's Journal.*

Bowen Dolhan
P.O. Box 848
Jasper, AB Canada T0E 1E0
780-852-3800
bmdolhan@telus.net

Bowen started guiding professionally in 1988 as an employee of Dave and Ellie Weins of Stone Mountain Safaris in northern British Columbia. He worked for them for eight years and in the process learned all the fundamentals of guiding; he then went to work for Scott Taylor of Bear Paw Outfitting. At that time he also got involved in late-season deer hunts, being partnered with Scott on this enterprise for ten years. He sold out his interest in 2005, but he's still guiding actively in northern British Columbia for late-season deer and in Alberta for mule deer.

He has personally guided more than four hundred hunters, although naturally not all of them for mule deer. He's guided for most species found in British Columbia, including sheep, mountain goat, grizzly and black bear, moose, caribou, wolf, elk, whitetail, and mule deer. Bowen has always hunted and trapped, and as a youngster his dream was to be a mountain guide. When he got the opportunity to do it, he simply fell in love with the job.

One of his biggest fascinations with guiding was learning his limitations—how far he could push himself and what he could and couldn't do. He's always loved being outdoors and seeing wild animals, so guiding became a natural offshoot for him. The challenge was even greater than that of hunting, though, because taking a client out after big game is a whole lot tougher. He has no specific reading recommendations, but picks up and reads almost any hunting magazine.

Ask the Mule Deer Guides

Harry Leuenberger
Baldy Mountain Outfitters
P.O. Box 42
Wardner, BC Canada V0B 2J0
250-429-3985
info@baldymountain.com
www.baldymountain.com

Harry started back in 1972 when he was only seventeen, so he has been at this business a long time. His dad had a guiding business, and when one of the guides got sick his dad desperately needed help. He took Harry out of school for three weeks to help, and that was the start of a stellar guiding career. Harry's still at it after all these years, and has personally guided almost two hundred fifty hunters.

He is fascinated by the life a guide leads. He's always loved the outdoors and always had an interest in both hunting and wildlife, so it's natural for him to take others out to hunt.

Harry is an avid reader and rates *One Man, One Rifle, One Land*, the author's publication, among his favorites. In recent years he has done a lot of sheep hunting and consequently likes *Grand Slam* and *Ovis* and just about any other magazine on sheep hunting.

Nick Frederick
Ameri-Cana Expeditions
6007-104 Street NW
Edmonton, AB Canada T6H 2K6
780-469-0579
www.ameri-cana.com
nick.frederick@shaw.ca

Nick graduated in 1992 with a degree in telecommunications from a technical institute in Edmonton, but after a year of working in that industry as a telephone company employee he decided he wanted a more satisfying career. In 1993, therefore, when he was twenty-three years old, Nick began guiding full time for his father, Pat Frederick of Ameri-Cana Expeditions, Inc. Pat, the head of the Frederick clan, has been guiding deer hunters for twenty-five years, and Nick's younger brother Dan has been guiding since 1991.

Currently he guides waterfowl hunters in September and October in Alberta, and then in November he guides hunters for deer and moose. He has personally guided about sixty deer hunters, which is about the same number as his brother. He loves to guide deer hunters because of the challenge—but also because it's part of his career.

Nick started hunting at a very young age and has hunted around the world, including the Northwest Territories, South Africa, Zimbabwe, Russia, Kazakhstan, Tajikistan, and Argentina. He lives in the city of Edmonton and says that he loves the great change when he heads out into the field and away from the rush of the city. As for reading material, he enjoys reading *Big Buck* magazine.

Ask the Mule Deer Guides

Mick Chapel
P.O. Box 291
Quemado, NM 87829
505-773-4599
www.nmtrophyhunts.com
jcchapel@wildblue.net

Mick is a man of few words who started guiding in New Mexico when he was about sixteen years old, some thirty years ago, and he's still guiding actively. He has no idea how many hunters he's taken afield, but he believes the number must be in the thousands. He does it mainly because he enjoys hunting, and it's a way to make a living doing what he likes best. These days he outfits hunts in Sonora for desert mule deer, leasing the best ranches he can find.

He shares many fresh insights in his interview for this book, and he has a unique way of putting things into perspective, especially regarding dealing with Mexico, its landowners, and its people. As far as reading is concerned, he doesn't read much on mule deer hunting. However, he readily admits to a personal fetish for hunting with hounds for some species, and he maintains a personal library containing a lot of old books about how old-timers hunted bears and lions right in his desert Southwest area a hundred years ago or more. Those kinds of books are Mick's favorites.

Eduardo Gomez Jr.
Explorer Safaris
Ave. Patria #600, Local 14-A
Col. Jardines Universidad,
C.P. 45110
Zapopan, Jalisco, Mexico
(011) 52-333-673-5110 or
(011) 52-333-673-1562
www.campfire.com.mx
eduardo@cexplorer.com.mx

Eduardo began his guiding career in 1989 on Fuente Clara, a ranch in Sonora, Mexico. He says that hunting was an absolute necessity at Fuente Clara, though over the years it has become more of a hobby for him. He still sometimes guides, but not very often, since he began his own company and its management requires much of his time. He will sometimes make an exception and guide someone who is after a truly exceptional mule deer. His main activities these days are promoting his company and attending to the business aspects of his operation. He does most of the hunt bookings and most of the promotion himself. He has personally guided about sixty hunters to desert mule deer.

He truly enjoys guiding and wishes that his business would allow him more time to do the "hands-on" aspect of guiding. He speaks and reads excellent English and likes books with more technical information on wildlife. He also likes the magazines published by Safari Club International and Ovis/Grand Slam.

Ask the Mule Deer Guides

David Lopez
c/o Jorge and Malena Camou
Sonora Adventures
(011) 52-662-216-9187
sonoradventus@yahoo.com.mx

David is a true anomaly in this book in that he has always been a working guide and cowboy with no aspirations (or opportunities) to move up in the guiding/outfitting business. He was recommended to me by Brent Sinclair, who calls him "one of the last of the truly great deer trackers in Mexico."

David speaks no English, so his interview was graciously conducted by Malena Camou; we followed the same questionnaire as was used with the other guides in the book. David was working as a cowboy in 1981 on one of the larger ranches now leased by Sonora Adventures when the ranch owner began bringing in hunters who wanted to take big desert mule deer. Nobody knew the ranch and its wildlife better than David, and that was his opportunity to start guiding hunters.

Although now in his sixties, he still actively guides hunters every year. He is modest about his tracking ability, but Brent Sinclair says that his feats are legendary—including the talent to sort out the tracks of a good desert muley from those of a herd of cows and sheep combined. He has guided more than five hundred hunters for all species, for mule deer as well as Coues whitetail, antelope, elk, and bighorn sheep.

David has always liked the outdoors and has particularly always liked to hunt. Being a guide allows him to be outdoors, doing what he truly loves. He reads any Spanish publication he can get on hunting, and he notes that there are quite a few such magazines available.

Chapter 2

SELECTING AN OUTFITTER/ GUIDE FOR MULE DEER

What should a hunter look for in an outfitter/guide?

Grant Adkisson: I think the first and foremost thing to look for is honesty. There are some great guides out there, and some great outfitters, but unfortunately there are also some guys whose sole motivation is to make money. They seldom have return clients, and they disappoint a lot of people. If possible, get character references and talk to people who have hunted with them. Try to find out what the outfitter and guide are like, and whether they have delivered on what they promised. Most hunters call and ask how big the bucks were that I killed last year, how big the largest buck I've ever taken was, or they ask for references for the biggest bucks. I tell our clients, instead, to ask for references from hunters who were not successful in taking a buck. Find out the circumstances involved and whether the outfitter was truthful with them about their chances. Ask whether they would go with him again, and whether he produced the kind of experience they were expecting. On our hunts we never guarantee anything but an honest effort: We try to undersell and then overproduce. I tell people who call me that they have a really good chance of killing a four-point buck or better, and almost all of them go home saying that the experience was far better than I'd portrayed it. That's the way I like it.

Jeff Chadd: I'd look for someone who has a good reputation, is honest, and runs a good hunt. He should reliably do what he tells you he's going to do, and his references should bear that out.

Robb Wiley: More than anything else, I'd seek someone who demonstrates enthusiasm and excitement about guiding. There are outfitters who have been in the business for many, many years who lose their edge. I'd look for an outfitter who is still sharp. When you find that, you've found one of the very best.

Spectacular Nevada scenery could be the deciding factor for some hunters. (Photo courtesy Thomas Brunson)

Keith Atcheson: The first considerations any hunter should have in choosing an outfitter/guide are experience, honesty, and integrity. There are a lot of "not so honest" people in the hunting and fishing business. It is truly a case of "buyer beware!" One good reference does not tell you much, but five or ten truly do if you are diligent and do your homework.

Doug Gardner: A hunter should be realistic when he's discussing a potential hunt with a guide or outfitter. If you're hearing exactly what you want to hear right down the line, beware! When people call me or stop by my booth at a sports show, and they tell me they really want to kill a Boone and Crockett mule deer, I tell them they have two chances: slim and none. Anybody that tells you differently is probably stretching the truth. If they're not, I'd like to hunt there! It's very important that an outfitter be honest with you and represent himself fairly in discussing his hunts. Here in eastern Montana, a key factor is how much hunting territory he has under his control, either by ownership or lease. That's not as big a factor in some other areas, where they're hunting big mountains and it's strictly public access. Here access is much too easy, with too many good roads. If the hunting isn't controlled by private interests the land gets hunted too hard, and there probably isn't much there.

Fred Lamphere: You should spend some time on the phone with the guide you're considering, and see if you can determine if you have a good personality match. You should then make it a priority to check references. Spend some time doing it and make sure you're making the right choice, because you're certainly going to spend some money.

Thomas Brunson: Honesty would be the top characteristic I'd seek. Beyond that, I'd find someone who spends a lot of time in the area and does a lot of preseason scouting, so they know what they've got and where to find it.

Troy Justensen: I'd look for experience over anything else. I'd also try to find someone with a good knowledge of the unit you'll be hunting, particularly here in Utah where most hunts are on a draw basis.

Jess Rankin: One thing any hunter needs to realize is that it doesn't matter so much what species you're hunting, there are several things to look for. The first is good game concentrations. Another is top-end trophy quality, and another is mild terrain that makes it easier to hunt—especially if your physical condition is poor or marginal. Finally, find out how easy it is to draw a tag, or, alternatively, how much a landowner tag costs. If you find an area with moderate terrain, good animals in high density, and excellent trophy quality, you can bet it isn't going to be inexpensive. Or if it's public land and a draw hunt, it isn't going to be easy to draw the tag. So for a first hunt, look for an outfitter who can offer the desired qualities at an affordable price. After you've had a good hunt of that type, look for an area and outfitter that offer the chance to get a really big deer. To do that, there are three possibilities: Look for an inexpensive outfitter in an area that might not have as many deer—and a consequently lower

Accommodations should be one consideration in choosing an outfitter and guide for mule deer. (Photo courtesy Robb Wiley)

chance of success—but that has the potential to produce a really big one. Alternatively, you can just get lucky and draw in a good area. The third possibility is to spend some money to hunt a really premium area, with a good chance of success on a really big mule deer.

Bowen Dolhan: I think that looking at references might be the most important thing. A reputable outfitter will share both good and bad references with a potential client—there are always some bad ones. The outfitter should be honest about that. It can be really important to talk to a hunter who has had a bad experience, whether the problem was the result of incompetence or neglect—or even if the cooking wasn't up to par. We always list both positive and negative references and are willing to send them to anyone who wants them. Some guides might not want to give those out, but we want potential clients to have a realistic look at our operation through the eyes of hunters we've served. Other important considerations are the history of the outfit, the percentage of successful hunters, as well as the trophy potential of the area. The number of years an outfitter has been in business can be important, too, because it's an indicator of experience. I'd never imply that there aren't some mighty good young outfitters and guides out there, though, and we all had our very first client hunter at some point.

Harry Leuenberger: That can be a fairly tough question, but near the top of my list would be honesty. The guide's reputation should tell the hunter a lot about what kind of person he is dealing with.

Nick Frederick: When looking for an outfitter you must look at many aspects of the operation. Some questions that you might want to ask would be: How long have they been in business? What state or province are they hunting, and exactly where are they located? Are they involved in the area's outfitting association?

Mick Chapel: I would look for someone with a lot of experience, as well as some honor and dignity. Those are hard qualities to recognize in an outfitter, but that's what you need. Most people initially talk to the outfitter on the phone about booking a hunt, and a lot of outfitters talk a pretty good line. Unfortunately, this business I've been in for most of my life seems to attract shysters more than any other business I know. All that unscrupulous people have to do is to persuade someone to send money for a hunting trip that may or may not be what it's cracked up to be. All other factors being equal, there's a better than 50 percent chance you'll get taken! And in Mexico, it's even worse than in the United States.

Eduardo Gomez Jr.: In an outfitter and guide, the hunter needs to look for someone that helps him to achieve the goal of finding a good trophy. Some tips would be to hunt in an area with a good population, good animal quality, and a good chance of success. Finally, the guide needs to give his hunter every possible advantage in trying to find a good animal.

David Lopez: An honest outfitter and guide should be the top priority.

What is the most important single characteristic of a good guide?

Grant Adkisson: Honesty is right at the top. Obviously woodsmanship, the ability to judge animals, and so on, are important, but if a guide is being deceitful with you, something major is going to go wrong. It doesn't matter how good a buck someone killed with a particular outfit last year. What counts is the overall quality of service they're able to deliver to all their clients. I've been with outfits that had a few pet clients that got into good hunting, while the rest of their hunters might never see an animal on a five-day hunt. Honesty and character are really important.

Jeff Chadd: People skills are very important. By that I mean how the guide handles and gets along with his clients.

Robb Wiley: I think it comes down to a passion for what the guide is doing. He's got to get up at 3:00 A.M., go to bed at midnight, and put in lots of twenty-hour days if he's going to be one of the best. To do that, you've got to be passionate about what you're doing. If you're not, fatigue, business pressures, and everything else will start to wear on you, and it will affect your job performance. It's raw, burning passion that gets you through trying times.

Keith Atcheson: The single most important characteristic of a good guide is patience. Actually, a good guide must have many characteristics, such as good eyesight, good physical conditioning, persistence, a good understanding of human nature, knowledge of the field care of trophies and meat, and being a good hunting companion. Above all, though, stands the human quality of patience. By it a guide can read his client as well as the game, and be very good at making the correct decision at the right time.

Doug Gardner: Everybody who comes here to hunt expects to be treated well, have a good time, and experience everything that's here to enjoy. I can teach a person to hunt and to guide, but if a guide doesn't have the ability to get along with others,

Televised hunt with outfitter Fred Lamphere, Lee Hursely, guide Rick Richard, and landowner Randy Fox. (Photo courtesy Fred Lamphere)

that's something I can't help. I think that people skill is the number one characteristic of a good guide.

Fred Lamphere: I believe it's the ability to listen to your hunter and know your hunter's abilities. That way you can plan a hunt that will be enjoyable and have the best chance of success.

Thomas Brunson: A guide has got to love what he's doing. He also needs a strong work ethic that puts the client first.

Troy Justensen: I'd stick with experience. That's the most important characteristic.

Jess Rankin: Being able to get along with hunters is even more important than being able to hunt deer. For one of my guides, I'd take a mediocre deer hunter who knows how to relate to people over some super hunting guy with no personality and no interest in others.

Bowen Dolhan: I'd have to say it would be an absolute passion for hunting and guiding.

Harry Leuenberger: I believe that a good work ethic and dedication to the task are the most important characteristics.

Ask the Mule Deer Guides

Nick Frederick: The most important characteristics are that he be a dedicated hunter himself, and that the guide holds a reputation for honesty and is very familiar with his hunting area.

Mick Chapel: A good guide has an uncanny ability to spot animals. There isn't even a close second to that. You can be driving down a road, and the guide will say, "Stop! There's a deer!"

For example, on a bighorn sheep hunt last year we were watching fourteen rams bedded on a big rock slide about four hundred yards away. We saw two other guys come by, a guide and a hunter from another outfitter, and they went almost to the rams and came all the way back. We could hear them talking, but they never even saw the sheep. You've got to have the eyes to see those animals, so you don't walk by the big one and never see it. The main reason people talk the talk but can't walk the walk is that they just don't have the eyes to spot the animals.

Eduardo Gomez Jr.: It's extremely important that the guide know very well the species you are hunting, and understand the animal's habits and behavior.

David Lopez: Good eyes and a good personality are important anywhere, but a guide's most outstanding characteristic in Sonora would be his ability to find and track big deer. It's also very important that he be able to tell a big deer from a small one.

What is the worst possible deficiency in a guide?

Grant Adkisson: I think it's the shyster mentality that tries to book as many clients each year as possible, regardless of the quality of the hunting experience. Such an operator realizes that none of his hunters will return the next year, but that doesn't matter: Next year there will be a bunch of new clients. Brochures and booths at hunting conventions can make things look great, but they can be deceptive, too. I recommend word-of-mouth referrals as the best source of information on a guide or outfitter because that's live, firsthand experience.

Jeff Chadd: Lack of people skills is the worst deficiency. If a guide can't even get along with his hunters, it's a major problem.

Female hunters are welcomed by most outfitters—and they do pretty darned well! (Photo courtesy Jess Rankin)

Robb Wiley: I have to say that the worst thing a guide could be is lazy.

Keith Atcheson: The worst possible deficiency in a hunting guide, in my opinion, is having little or no respect for their client or the game they are pursuing. Additionally, the guide who tries to beat his client into the ground to prove he is more physically fit is the guide that needs to be released by the outfitter as soon as possible. Other deficiencies would include being abusive toward stock or other employees, using foul language, drinking excessively, or openly talking in negative fashion about past clients.

Doug Gardner: The worst deficiency would be a lack of people skills and the inability to get along with others.

Fred Lamphere: Pushing a hunter beyond his physical capabilities can lead to disaster, so it's a major deficiency.

Thomas Brunson: It's a major deficiency when a guide reaches the point of burnout and loses enthusiasm for the

Spartan accommodations are often necessary to reach the best mule deer hunting. Note the giant antlers in the background. (Photo courtesy Thomas Brunson)

work. If a guide's motivation is simply to make money, he's doing it for the wrong reasons. Not that there's a whole lot of money in this business, by most standards, but if you've got money on your mind you can get into all kinds of unethical practices to increase the bottom line. You want to avoid that kind of person.

Troy Justensen: Inexperience is the worst thing I can think of. A guide who can't offer at least a measure of experience ought to be doing something else.

Jess Rankin: Since I believe getting along with people is the most important attribute of a good guide, the converse is also true. Hunters get mighty tired of hearing guides that talk only about themselves and what they're all about. I'd much rather have somebody who's fun to be with, even if their hunting skills are a cut below. I've got a girl who guides for me, and she's originally from Germany. She's been working for me for about twenty-five years, and she's a mule deer hunting fanatic! She gets her hunters more big mule deer than anyone. I've got as many as twenty-five guides working for me sometimes, and she's tops!

Bowen Dolhan: I think the worst deficiency is a lack of respect for the hunter. It's all too common to hear outfitters and guides talking down their hunters behind their backs. You can sometimes spot such people at shows when they talk critically about past clients, rather than being positive and welcoming to all. The client is paying their way, and yet they aren't respectful of that relationship, and it shows in their work. They aren't 100 percent committed to the hunter, so he doesn't get their full effort.

Harry Leuenberger: I'd have to say that laziness or disorganization would be pretty close to the worst deficiencies.

Nick Frederick: The biggest deficiency in a guide is being unfamiliar with the area and having no drive or ambition to go the extra mile for the client.

Mick Chapel: I consider dishonesty the worst deficiency, and I simply won't tolerate it in a guide. If they're not telling you the truth, they can lead the whole camp astray and do a lot of harm. You've got to be able to trust what a guide says. My trust in people who work for me comes from knowing them for a long time and being certain they're honest.

Eduardo Gomez Jr.: The worst guide would be the one who is impatient and pushes the hunter to shoot, even when the situation isn't right. It's also pretty bad when the guide doesn't know the area and the species well enough to conduct an efficient and effective hunt.

David Lopez: It's a major deficiency if the guide isn't able to walk quietly for a long ways, and if he doesn't have good eyes for glassing and finding deer.

Some people say all the big mule deer are gone. What do you say about this?

Grant Adkisson: We're now living in some of the greatest years of mule deer hunting since the 1960s. On our ranch and a couple of ranches where I hunted in the 1960s, I've taken some of my best mule deer, including three over 190. We went through a time when mule deer were hurting and we weren't seeing the number and quality of bucks we had seen before. Now that has really turned around. One of our biggest problems was mountain lions, which have increased greatly in number in recent years. They continue to take a huge number of deer, but I still think we're seeing more big muley bucks than we have in many years. For one thing, we've started hunting more places away from the main mountain lion areas, such as the plains and the mountain area around Gunnison. The point restrictions and other good management moves are also helping. Another huge factor is the increased value of the wildlife resource, because anytime the value increases, as it has with mule deer, the resource is more appreciated and better protected. Some people complain about the cost of a quality mule deer hunt, but the fact that the value is there is a major reason big deer are available.

Jeff Chadd: There's no way all the big ones are gone! They're still here, but you have to look a little harder to find them. Here in Colorado they've done a really good job of managing mule deer, and now all deer are on a drawing basis. Mule deer have come back great guns, and there are some tremendous bucks around. Last year the average score for the sixteen muley bucks I took in Colorado was 188, and I took three over 200. We've got good country and good mule deer, if they don't ruin it by increasing the number of tags so it's not sustainable.

Robb Wiley: I disagree that there are no big muleys around. There may be fewer of them and they're certainly harder to find, but there are still huge muley bucks out there. You've just got to know where to look, you've got to be patient, and, obviously, you've got to cover a lot more country than in the old days.

Keith Atcheson: That may be true for some areas, but we're still seeing plenty of big bucks. It all depends on the management regimen, such as how many tags the state issues, and private landowners limiting the numbers of bucks taken off their property. The genetics and the food sources are still there, but you can't shoot small bucks if you want them to grow to be big bucks.

Doug Gardner: I think there was a heyday of mule deer hunting in the past, when there were fewer hunters and bucks

Finding big muleys is a summertime scouting job much of the time. (Photo courtesy Bowen Dolhan)

had a chance to get older. But that being said, hunting on the big ranches we lease has improved dramatically. We've done it by limiting hunting pressure and exercising good-quality management, so the deer have a chance to grow old. The natural good genetics in our deer are another factor. I think that a good mule deer hunt is one of the harder things to find, especially on public land, which often is adjacent to private winter range that's being developed. If you can find a hunt where that isn't a problem, and the outfitter has enough land under his control, you can still find big muley bucks.

Fred Lamphere: I might have agreed with that statement ten to fifteen years ago, but in my own lifetime I've seen our mule deer coming back in a big way. It's because of a number of factors, but chief among them is rancher education. I've had a ranch leased here in Butte County, South Dakota, and the quality has gone up every year. It's because of good management and limiting the harvest. Other factors have been hunting videos and satellite television, which have made people, and especially ranchers, a lot more aware of the benefits of wildlife management. I don't think the big muley bucks are all gone. I think they're coming back stronger than ever.

Thomas Brunson: Maybe that's true in some areas of the country, but here in Nevada mule deer hunting is better than when I was a kid. I think it's on the upswing. In some areas there aren't as many big deer as there were twenty years ago, but in most places it's at least holding its own. I've seen more big bucks here in the last few years than during all my growing up years combined. The reason is a combination of factors, including the fact that we've had several wet years in a row, which is unusual for Nevada. Also, the game department has cut back a lot on the number of permits issued. They're taking a very conservative approach to mule deer management, and that's really helped bring them back.

Troy Justensen: I don't think that's right. Sure, overall numbers are down throughout the West, but there are several units that had been shut down completely that are now producing phenomenal mule deer. Some of the things that are being done, such as habitat restoration and improvement, are starting to show results. There's also effective predator control being carried out in some Western states. I think you're going to see a big rebound in mule deer quality across the entire West over the next several years.

Jess Rankin: I don't know if that's right or not. You look at what Colorado has done by putting their deer tags on a drawing statewide. One of my guides from up that way says he's never seen a comeback like the one their mule deer have made. He went hunting last fall and says he saw more deer than when he was a kid. He killed a buck that grossed 180, and he hunted only three days. New Mexico put deer tags on a statewide drawing in 2005, which is eventually going to help a lot. They had been adding more limited entry zones, but what that did was force the general license holders to hunt on smaller and smaller pieces of the state. They cut the number of tags to about half of what they'd sold over the counter the year before, and we're starting to see more good deer. We've had some good wet years lately, and that's helping fawn survival. I believe that in two or three years you're going to see more bucks in an older age class. It's got a ways to go, but I think we're headed in the right direction. That's not true all over New Mexico, though, because in the southwestern part of the state there are very few mule deer left. Still, they continue to issue too many tags, in my opinion.

Bowen Dolhan: I don't think that's true at all, especially here in Alberta. It may be true in some areas, but not here. With the trophy management program that the province brought in some years ago, the deer are continually getting bigger. Before that anyone could go in and buy a buck tag, but now all buck tags are on a draw basis. The result is that we're producing real trophies because we've got a population with a good age-class of trophies.

Harry Leuenberger: It's not the case in our area. We did have a really bad winter in 1996 with a significant die-off, but the management regimen has been changed since then and the really big bucks are coming back in a big way. The new regimen includes reducing the antlerless take and changing to a four-point restriction for the entire season. That means a buck must have at least four points on one side. This has given more bucks a chance to get to the necessary age to reach full potential.

Nick Frederick: Alberta is a sleeping giant when it comes to mule deer. In many parts of the province world-class bucks have been taken every year for approximately the past twelve years. For some reason Alberta doesn't get the press that other mule deer areas do. It appears we are beginning to be noticed, though, since outfitters in the good areas are becoming booked up early. If someone says there are no big mule deer out there, they probably haven't been to Alberta. Our resident draw system has been in place now for a dozen years, and the hunting gets better and better every year. Alberta has been famous for white-tailed deer for many years, and most hunters that come on a mule deer hunt also have a whitetail tag, just in case a big buck shows himself.

Mick Chapel: Perhaps there aren't as many as there used to be, but there are still plenty of them out there. Despite the fact that all the hunting is done during the rut, Sonora will never be hunted out because it has a huge population of mule deer that are completely unhuntable. There are some areas that are pancake flat and so thick you can't see thirty yards. If they haven't been prepared like some of the best ranches, by opening up large areas of brush with a bulldozer and seeding the open places with grass, you just can't hunt there at all. You can maybe put someone on a high rack on the back of a truck and do a little hunting, but for the most part there's no way to take mule deer out of such a tangle. There's certainly no way you're going to shoot all the big ones.

Eduardo Gomez Jr.: I think we still have good mule deer in the field, but unfortunately not everything is going so well, at least in Sonora. In my opinion mule deer are being overhunted there, and right now it can be very difficult to find a good trophy.

David Lopez: There are still some big deer, but not as many as in years past. You just have to work harder to find them.

Why do you think mule deer are being displaced from much of their original range by whitetails? Is this a problem in your area?

Grant Adkisson: I've seen the phenomenon be a problem to the east of us, more out on the plains. In our area around Gunnison it isn't much of a problem. I was really shocked the first time I saw a young 17-inch-wide white-tailed buck whip a 27- to 28-inch mule deer buck by whacking him in the side and running him off from a group of about nine mule deer does. That little whitetail then came back and proceeded to breed one of the does! We certainly know that mule deer bucks fight, but for some reason whitetails intimidate mule deer bucks and seem to dominate them. It results in the end in mule deer being pushed out of at least some areas they have formerly inhabited.

Jeff Chadd: It's not a problem at all for me because my Colorado hunts are conducted way up in the high country, between eight thousand and twelve thousand feet. There are no whitetails up there!

The results of just ten days of hunting in Alberta. (Photo courtesy Bowen Dolhan)

Robb Wiley: We don't have the problem with whitetails that exists in other places. More than anything we've got an elk issue, where elk are competing directly with mule deer on the winter range and the mule deer are losing. The issue of decreasing mule deer isn't from any one source; it's a multiple-factor issue. We've got winter range encroachment by the oil and gas industry in Wyoming, and we've got subdivisions and home development on wintering grounds in Idaho, as well as loss of habitat to agricultural interests. Also, in our area especially, predators play a huge role. My family homesteaded in southeastern Idaho many, many years ago, in an area known to have the best mule deer genetics in the whole country. When my father was a boy, if they saw two coyote tracks all winter it was considered amazing. Now I can go to those same areas in winter on a snowmobile and kill seven to ten coyotes in a single day. So coyotes, mountain lions, and these other factors are probably much more important than whitetail encroachment.

Ask the Mule Deer Guides

Keith Atcheson: Some of that doubtless occurs, but it doesn't seem to be the problem we once thought it might be. It's affected our areas very little.

Doug Gardner: It's really not a problem in our area, even though the two species coexist here. They require different bedding grounds, although they often feed on the same fields. Whitetails are mainly down on the river bottoms, while the mule deer are up on higher ground. Whitetails are more aggressive animals that take the bedding grounds they want; the muleys move on and take someplace else. But displacement of mule deer hasn't been a problem here, and it's fairly rare to see a whitetail-mule deer cross. Elk are more of a problem because when there are too many elk, the mule deer can't compete for food and will leave. Mountain lions are also a problem, because deer will move out when a lion comes through. I think that mule deer are the mainstay of the diet of most lions, not elk or whitetails.

Fred Lamphere: We're in what we call the tri-state area of South Dakota, and our western border is Montana to the north and Wyoming to the south. Our mule deer are really holding their own with the whitetails. Whitetails are always aggressive and you're not going to take that away from them, but there are natural factors that tend to control the spread of whitetails. For example, blue tongue is a disease that kills whitetails, while mule deer have a natural immunity. The end result is that in our area we don't have a problem with whitetails displacing mule deer.

Thomas Brunson: It's certainly not a problem in Nevada, because we have no whitetails. What I've read seems to indicate that where there are whitetails they're more aggressive than muleys, and they thrive in a wider range of habitats. Mule deer pretty much must have browse, whereas whitetails are more able to use a variety of food sources. Here in Nevada, mule deer compete more with elk, and Dr. Valerius Geist wrote an article demonstrating that elk can actually displace mule deer in places where there is a big elk concentration. Still, I'm kind of on the fence about that, because elk are primarily grazers and mule deer are browsers. I've seen them feeding in the same places, with mule deer right in among the elk.

Troy Justensen: We don't have a significant whitetail population in Utah, and in fact whitetails aren't even recognized as a species here as far as the game department is concerned. Therefore they don't have any substantial impact on mule deer. However, in some units elk populations are burgeoning, and I believe that elk do without question displace mule deer. When the elk and mule deer are forced onto the same winter range, the mule deer have a hard time competing and can suffer as a result.

Jess Rankin: I don't think that's a big problem, because I've hunted a lot in places where mule deer and whitetails are ranging together. I can count on the fingers of one hand the number of times I've seen a cross-breed. The first one I ever saw was killed by one of my hunters out in west Texas, and I'll elaborate on that in the "unusual stories" section. The point is that such an animal is indeed unusual, so it can't be a big problem for mule deer.

Bowen Dolhan: It's not much of a problem in our area, although I've heard of its being an issue elsewhere. There are a couple of reasons why we aren't experiencing that problem, I think. Sometimes there can be competition for available food, and whitetails are definitely more aggressive. Where I am we've got plenty for both kinds of deer—lots more feed than either kind of deer would ever need. Also, mule deer don't like being around whitetails because whitetails are so much more skittish. Mule deer are a lot more relaxed than whitetails, and mule deer don't like that nervous attitude. We often see whitetails and mule deer in the same fields, even feeding right beside each other, but mule deer definitely seem not to like being around whitetails. In certain areas you'll get whitetails that are being skittish for some reason, and the mule deer will move off because they can't handle it. But overall, whitetails displacing or reducing the numbers of mule deer hasn't been a problem.

Harry Leuenberger: It's not a concern in our area at this time. We see mule deer and whitetails close together all year-round, but intermingling is rare. We do see the occasional cross, but those are certainly unusual. I know that Dr. Valerius Geist has said in one of his books that mule deer are eventually going

Shed hunting is a reliable indicator of the quality of bucks in an area. (Photo courtesy Bowen Dolhan)

to become extinct because of whitetail encroachment, but we haven't seen any evidence of that so far. Both species seem to be doing quite well.

Nick Frederick: The displacement of mule deer does not occur to any significant degree in our area. Mule deer numbers are so high that it's not possible. However, I can see how that could be a problem in some areas, especially if the habitat is marginal for mule deer. Even here it isn't uncommon to see white-tailed bucks running with mule deer does.

Mick Chapel: It is a problem in New Mexico, where mule deer have disappeared in some areas. The issue is not just whitetails, though, but also heavy competition from elk and domestic stock. The federal land grazing here is the least expensive in the world, averaging $1.25 per animal per month. If you want to lease private land to run your cattle on, it's going to cost you $14 to $16 a month per head. Federal land is dirt cheap, and consequently it's grossly overgrazed. That's typical of government oversight and management, which almost always equals mismanagement.

Overgrazing leads to all the grass being eaten first, and when cattle finish with the grass they move on to the browse species, such as chemise, mountain mahogany, and cliff rose. Mule deer simply must have that browse. I've seen cattle up in steep, brushy country, and they haven't just nibbled the end of the brush. They eat it back to where it's a quarter-inch in diameter! They're biting it off to where it's the size of a pencil! In some places they're killing critical species like chemise, and the mule deer inevitably suffer. That's another reason mule deer do so well in Sonora—there's just not any grass at all here, except where they plant it after the bulldozer does its work. It's all shrubs and cactus, and the mule deer love that. The private ranches in New Mexico still have great mule deer hunting because they take care of the habitat and they don't overgraze it. But where there's overgrazing, it's natural for mule deer to decline. Now they're putting wolves in New Mexico, and it's putting more pressure on mule deer. They're even thinking of putting grizzly bears back in this country. My God, we just finished a very successful extermination program to get rid of those unwanted predators and tame the land, and now they're putting them back! It's like putting rats back into the barn.

Eduardo Gomez Jr.: In Sonora, mule deer habitat is very different from Coues deer habitat, so there is no displacement. The two species have survived for centuries without any conflict.

David Lopez: This is not a problem with desert mule deer. They inhabit the same areas as Coues deer but tend to live lower on the mountain. Coues deer may not be as aggressive as other whitetails in displacing desert mule deer, either.

Chapter 3

MULE DEER GUIDES EVALUATE THE HUNTER

What is your favorite type of hunter (personality, physical abilities, experience level, socioeconomic status)?

Grant Adkisson: Some categories don't matter at all. Personality, though, is very important, because a good personality often breeds a positive attitude. I like someone who appreciates being out in God's creation and enjoys seeing what has been made. Even a person with a physical disability can have a positive viewpoint and enjoy being out in the mountains, taking in the beautiful aspen trees in fall, and seeing some animals. Such a person will usually look upon killing an animal as just another plus to the experience and be appreciative of what the guide and outfitter are doing for them, of the country that God has created—and of just getting to hunt. That's my favorite kind of hunter. I've guided some of the biggest names on the national scene, and people who own some of the big sports franchises who are exceedingly rich. I've guided others who have saved for fifteen years to be able to do such a hunt. I enjoy all of them, so long as their attitude is positive and they're not taking the experience for granted.

Jeff Chadd: I like a guy who really wants to hunt and is here to enjoy the country, the experience, and the camaraderie. I don't like guiding the guy who's here just to be a killer.

Robb Wiley: Without a doubt my favorite is the guy who shows up with a positive attitude and a determination to have a good time. He might have a dream of a huge mule deer, but that's not his primary motivation. A hunter like that is determined to enjoy himself and give 100 percent on the hunt, regardless of the shape he's in. When it's the last hour of the last day, he's just as enthusiastic as on the first hour of the first day. That's a great

Are you in good enough shape to get up where this giant buck lived? (Photo courtesty Troy Justensen)

quality, because we've hit some real home runs in the last hours of a hunt. More than anything, believing in it long enough that it happens is what it takes to be successful on big mule deer.

Keith Atcheson: My favorite type of hunter is someone that allows me to do the job for which they've hired me. Hunters who are willing to listen and follow my lead and not question every decision I make are my favorite people to guide. If a hunter is in decent to good physical condition that helps greatly, but even hunters who are in poor shape have a great opportunity to take game if they listen to their guide.

Doug Gardner: Personality is really high on my list. I like a hunter who's truly interested in the hunt itself but also likes the history of the ranches and the area, the people, the animals—the hunter who wants to go out and see it all. I like people who appreciate what we've done and what we have. Socioeconomic status doesn't even enter the picture. We treat everyone the same. In camp it doesn't matter whether a hunter is the CEO or the janitor. Physical limitations are fine, too, so long as people can accept the situation as it is. We've taken people in wheelchairs, and they've been successful. We've taken the opposite end of the spectrum, too—the fit, young person who wants to put on a backpack and hunt that way. But that also has its downside. You can't cover as much of this vast prairie land on foot as you can by vehicle.

Fred Lamphere: I like a hunter who has studied the area and knows what to expect. Also, I really like it when a hunter enjoys the hunt more than the kill.

Thomas Brunson: I like hunters who are looking to hunt as hard as I do, or at least are willing to hunt up to the limit of their physical ability. It's awesome to have someone show up who's in great physical shape and can go wherever I can. I also like someone who's willing to listen. I really had problems with that when I first started, because I was young and guiding a lot of hunters who were much older than I. They'd tend to question my calls on various aspects of the hunt—at least until they'd spent a few days with me and figured out that I knew what I was doing. Physical ability is important, but experience level isn't, as long as the hunter is willing to listen to me. Socioeconomic status doesn't matter, because I've guided rich guys who have it all, and I've guided people who have saved for years to be able to come on a guided hunt. Most of them, at either end of the spectrum or in between, are really good people, but I've had some bad eggs, too.

Troy Justensen: I don't know if I can pinpoint it to any one characteristic, but I certainly like the ones who have a real passion for hunting. Some outfitters don't like to take bow hunters, but I really enjoy them because I like to get in close. Some guides don't like taking women, but again, it's a challenge I accept and enjoy. I sometimes guide the wives of our hunters, and it's really a thrill to get them involved and help them, in many cases, to take their first animal. And some of the most memorable hunts I've been in on, and some of the most rewarding, have been with disabled kids, some of them in wheelchairs.

Would this boy be enough to give you buck fever? (Photo courtesy Bowen Dolhan)

Jess Rankin: I'd obviously like a thirty-year-old marathon runner with deep pockets who's willing to pass up 170-inch deer looking for a 180 or bigger! Unfortunately, you don't get very many like that. Seriously, I like a hunter who realizes that hunting is hunting and that nothing outside a fence is guaranteed. Good physical conditioning is always a plus, but some of our hunts, such as our mule deer hunts in west Texas, are pretty easy because we mostly just high-rack hunt from a pickup truck. Mainly I like realistic expectations. I go after and attract a lot of experienced hunters who have a lot of hunts behind them, and that always helps, too.

Bowen Dolhan: My favorite type is the hunter who enjoys the hunt as much as, or more than, the kill. I really like guys who are just extremely happy to be out there, and who give it 100 percent all the time. They make the most of every day, whether the weather is good or bad, or even whether you're seeing deer or not.

Harry Leuenberger: Personality and physical ability are probably the most important in hunting our area. Experience isn't a big deal: That's why the hunter hired a guide in the first place, at least in part. Socioeconomic status doesn't matter to me, either. I like a guy with some personality who enjoys being out with the guide and who has the physical ability to get to the deer when we find the one we want.

Nick Frederick: First-time mule deer hunters are great. They are generally serious hunters who have traveled far to try to kill a good buck, so they are not going to shoot the first little buck that comes along. They tend to be more likely to take the guide's advice on which buck to kill. Too many times, hunters have not trusted their guide's judgment on a buck and have either gone home disappointed or taken a lesser buck. Sometimes it seems that they just want to be the one who makes the decision. It's very enjoyable to guide hunters who come on a hunt to spend time away from work, to relax, and to revel in the outdoors. The hunter who puts 110 percent focus on the deer hunt itself can sometimes be more difficult to guide, although at the end of the day it's not usually a problem.

Mick Chapel: I like somebody who can shoot! That's the worst problem we have in hunting all species, including mule deer: Ninety percent of hunters can't shoot! Most of the time the guys who get the big ones make a really nice shot, but too many hunters these days aren't capable of it. I was hunting the Jicarilla Reservation with a guy several years ago, and we saw a giant mule deer up ahead, exactly 368 yards away. All you could see were the antlers, head, and neck. That guy knelt down beside a little old spindly tree, and when he fired that buck jumped six feet off the ground. We ran up, and the deer hadn't gone twenty yards. It was a huge mule deer, and it was stone dead. That's the difference between hero and zero! Another time, I pushed a huge deer out over a guy into a big open space where I had him sitting, and he fired six times at that deer at 75 yards, missing every time. It ruined his whole hunt because he just couldn't make the shot. He missed the deer of a lifetime! Unfortunately, that kind of thing happens 80 percent of the time, even when it's a chip shot. Physical ability is a part of it, but it's not nearly as important as being able to shoot!

Stay cool and collected and he just might be yours! (Photo courtesy
Bowen Dolhan)

Ask the Mule Deer Guides

Eduardo Gomez Jr.: I like guiding someone who is patient and quiet by nature. You don't necessarily need to be an athlete to be a successful desert mule deer hunter.

David Lopez: I enjoy guiding a hunter who is patient and in good physical condition, so he can walk all day. My personal favorite is the one who has more interest in the hunt than in the kill, and a hunter who will follow my instructions instead of going off on his own.

What is the most challenging kind of hunter, and why?

Grant Adkisson: On a few occasions I've had hunters who don't even notice the beautiful scenery or appreciate being in the great outdoors. One of the worst examples was a young man whose father had paid for the hunt, and on his first hunt he took a very nice 340 bull elk, a great trophy. He hardly said anything about it. He came back a few years later with his father, and that particular year I had found a real monster elk. It just so happened that the boy and I got on that bull, and he killed it. It was one of the most magnificent animals you can imagine, scoring around 390. The kid walked up to it, and the first thing he said was, "Well, I don't know what I'm going to do with this thing. The other one I killed my dad got mounted, and it's stored in the garage." He had no appreciation at all for the incredible animal. To me, that's the biggest challenge in guiding. I've guided two Alzheimer's victims, and they didn't even remember shooting an animal. But at least they had good attitudes and there was appreciation.

Jeff Chadd: To me, that would be the guy who's out of shape so badly it spoils his hunt. We might see a tremendous buck, but it doesn't do him any good because we can't get him to it.

Robb Wiley: The most challenging kind would have to be the one who comes with huge expectations and is very demanding. There are a lot of magazine articles and videos about mule deer hunting these days, and the way they're produced feeds that kind of attitude. The media people put out things like "The Top 100 Muley Bucks of All Time." Hunters see and read this stuff and they come to camp thinking it's going to be easy to get a buck like that. They think they deserve such a trophy simply because they've hired an outfitter, but they're not willing to put in the work required to get the job done. A person who has bought into that disturbing mindset is the most challenging hunter to me.

Keith Atcheson: The most challenging type of hunter to guide, in my opinion, is the client that is unsafe with firearms. There is nothing more important than safety in the field with firearms. Unfortunately, each year we have clients that are not always 100 percent aware of where their barrel is pointed. The greatest risk any guide faces in the field is being shot by a client. In my opinion, there is no reason ever to load a rifle until you are actually ready to shoot. Certain types of hunting may require having a chambered round and the safety on, but in most cases you shouldn't chamber a round until you are ready to shoot. My father's best friend was shot and killed by a client many years ago in a hunting accident that was the result of pure negligence and inexperience on the client's part. We've had several close calls over the years in our own guiding experience, and it is something a good guide never forgets. More importantly, it's something the client should never forget.

Doug Gardner: For us, the most challenging kind is the hunter who is not realistic and is very demanding. I could come up with a list of negative personality traits that I wouldn't want to see again. It's the kind of person who thinks that, simply because he's booked with a guide who has a huge amount of land leased and has lots of experience, he's going to kill a Boone and Crockett deer! Most of the time that isn't going to happen. That's true of whatever big-game species you're hunting, but it's especially true of mule deer. We can show people a lot of different bucks in a week's time, but the odds of one of them measuring up as ideal are slim. No matter how much you tell people that, some come with the idea that I've got a 195-inch mule deer hidden somewhere around the corner, and if they're demanding enough I'll show it to them. That makes for a long week.

Fred Lamphere: It's really challenging when hunters come here with a number they expect their mule deer to meet,

Getting into and out of tough mule deer country can tax you to the limit. Are you ready? (Photo courtesy Thomas Brunson)

whether it's 180, 190, or whatever. Those are the hunters who are tough, especially if they're really rigid about it, to the point that they can't find contentment unless it's met. I've had a lot of hunters, though, who come with a high goal, but when they see something they really like in a mature buck they take that animal and are happy with their decision. I don't have a problem with goal-setting, and if you're willing to be flexible, it can be a real plus. Bucks that score 190 are so rare that it's not going to happen on many hunts, and a guy shouldn't have a goal so high that it ruins the enjoyment of the hunt.

Thomas Brunson: That would be the know-it-all that you can't tell anything. Such people think they already know everything. Usually, physically challenged hunters aren't that way, even though they take some special consideration and extra time. At least they'll listen to you and do what it takes to be successful.

Troy Justensen: That's got to be the guy who really can't afford the guide he's hired, but he's read all the books about hunting yet has lost touch with the reality that hunting is just that—hunting, not killing. There's a vital element of uncertainty, or it isn't really hunting. Sometimes no matter what you do, it just doesn't work out. So for me the most challenging hunter is the one who can't afford not to be successful, because he's hired a guide even though he can't afford one. Unless his hunt is picture-perfect, he's not going to be satisfied.

Jess Rankin: I'd say it's the guy who thinks that because he's paid money for the hunt he's automatically entitled to kill a big buck. His attitude is that if he doesn't get one, it's someone else's fault and not his own. You get the occasional hunter, maybe one out of twenty, who's the kind of guy who thinks that if he's not successful, it's because the guide screwed up.

Bowen Dolhan: The hunter with a negative attitude is the most challenging to me. It's tough enough to kill a real trophy buck, and someone who's got a poor attitude makes it just that much more difficult. Hunters like that are always saying they're not lucky, or we're never going to be able to do it—and all of a sudden the guide's got to become a shrink at the same time he's a guide. A guide has got enough to worry about without having to keep his hunter pumped up all the time.

Harry Leuenberger: I'm really stressed by the overly aggressive hunter who wants to be constantly on the move and wants to tell you what to do on the hunt. Hunters like that are not patient enough to sit and glass so you can find the big buck you want.

Nick Frederick: The most challenging hunters to guide are the ones that become very depressed when they go a couple of days and don't see a good deer. They can end up pouting, complaining, and just making everyone miserable. An attitude like that is not only hard for a guide to take but also can bring down a whole deer camp's enthusiasm. There is no room for negative people or crybabies in deer camp.

Mick Chapel: I think I've already answered that question. The most challenging kind of hunter is the one who just can't shoot. I had a sick hunter once who wanted to go back to camp, and we were five hours back in the bush. On the way we came up to an open area where I spotted a huge muley buck asleep under a cedar tree, less than three hundred yards away. I got the guy off the horse and got him set up, but his rifle barrel was waving all over the place. I knew he was going to miss, so I stopped him, took out my pocket knife, and whittled off the branches of the little tree we were hiding behind. I made him a really solid rest in the middle of the tree. Then I told him to shoot, and he did, but nothing happened! The next time he fired the deer jumped up and just stood there in the shade, not knowing what was happening. The third shot hit the deer but it was in the guts, and we had to chase it down to kill it. When we got the deer, we found that the hunter's second shot had blown a hole right through the antlers, right where the bottom fork is located. Poor shooting is a major challenge, no matter what you're hunting, and the problem seems to be getting worse. The poorest shooters are always the guys who walk into camp telling you they can shoot the eyes out of a gnat at a thousand yards. Watch out when a guy brags about his shooting ability, because he's the one who will always miss!

Eduardo Gomez Jr.: It can be very demanding to guide someone who already has a really good mule deer and wants a bigger one. Guiding such a hunter requires a lot of patience, and the hunter should plan on doing at least two hunts to achieve their goal.

David Lopez: The most challenging hunters for me are the ones in poor physical condition who won't listen to what I tell them.

Does it take any special characteristic to be a good mule deer hunter that might not apply to other types of deer hunting?

Grant Adkisson: Your physical persistence has to be pretty good. I'm amazed at some whitetail hunters who are able to sit such long hours in a stand. That kind of persistence is very important to being a successful mule deer hunter. This is big country, and it's necessary to cover a lot of it in a hunt. Some mule deer hunters become discouraged too easily and tend to give up.

Jeff Chadd: The high country is really a different kind of hunt, because it's so much a glassing hunt. A hunter needs to

When you're prepared, the payoff can be the hunt of a lifetime. (Photo courtesy Thomas Brunson)

be in above-average shape, but also be patient with glassing. In whitetail hunting you're probably sitting in a stand with limited visibility, so you expect to have to be patient. In our wide-open country, there's a temptation to want to look around the next ridge instead of staying put and doing the work of glassing.

Robb Wiley: It takes believing in it longer and being extremely persistent. In other types of deer hunting, you might see more animals more quickly, but with mule deer you've sometimes got to be really patient before you see a good buck.

Keith Atcheson: Most mule deer hunting is very similar in that almost all of it is done by spotting and stalking. One of the most important characteristics of a good mule deer hunter is great patience in glassing areas that might hold big deer. Being able to read tracks is important, too, as is being particularly familiar with the entire hunting area. There is no substitute for experience.

Doug Gardner: I don't think so, because what it takes to hunt mule deer also applies to other species. In some ways it's a little different, perhaps, especially for a do-it-yourself hunter. It takes exceptional optics and exceptional knowledge of the terrain, so you know where to look. It also takes a lot of patience if you're going to find a great trophy.

Fred Lamphere: In a word, it takes patience.

Thomas Brunson: Yes, a mule deer hunter must be extremely patient while glassing. You've got to be able to sit in one spot for hours and pick it all apart in order to find the animal you're looking for. If you get overly impatient during this phase of the hunt, you may not be successful.

Troy Justensen: Patience really stands out as important. There aren't a lot of really big mule deer in North America, probably fewer than any other major game species, so it's probably the most difficult animal to get and the most sought-after trophy. If you're trying to find that buck of a lifetime, it may take several trips, so both patience and persistence are important.

Jess Rankin: Not really. If you want a big mule deer, you've got to be willing to pass up smaller bucks, but that's the same with other deer hunting.

Bowen Dolhan: In our area, we do a lot of spot-and-stalk hunting, so it's pretty important that hunters know how to conduct themselves on a stalk. We've walked away from lots of deer because things weren't right to put a good, effective stalk on the animal. The hunter needs to understand the principles of stalking and why sometimes it's necessary to come back another day. Just because you can see the deer doesn't mean you can always get in position to take it.

Harry Leuenberger: As I mentioned before, it takes a lot of patience to be able to sit for long periods and glass until you find what you're seeking. That may apply to lots of other kinds of hunting, too, but with mule deer hunting you've got to be especially patient and willing to wait for your opportunity. It may take many hours behind the binoculars to accomplish this. With mule deer, you just never know when they're going to pop up.

Nick Frederick: As with most deer hunting, patience is very important. While hunting mule deer with me, the hunter usually has many opportunities to observe mule deer for hours on end. With that in mind, patience is a virtue, because you can be tempted to give up finding a big one and take something less.

Mick Chapel: There's not really any special characteristic, especially if you're purchasing guided hunts. The biggest thing is to hire a really good guide who can put you onto good animals. A good hunter is actually going to help the guide, and he's going to spot some of the animals himself. Any hunt should be a team effort between the guide and the hunter, because teamwork greatly increases the chances of success.

Eduardo Gomez Jr.: A good hunter is a good hunter. I don't believe hunting desert mule deer takes any special qualifications.

David Lopez: For hunting desert mule deer in Sonora, the hunter must be a very good walker, and it helps to be able to walk all day. Some days we cover many miles on foot, and if the hunter isn't able to do that it certainly reduces the chance of success.

How important is it that the hunter be physically fit to hunt mule deer with you?

Grant Adkisson: I've guided one man of eighty-seven years on a successful mule deer hunt, so not everybody needs to be in top physical shape. That said, it sure helps to have persistence, whether you're in great shape or not. All hunters should be amenable to letting the guide push them a little to their level of endurance, whatever that might be. It's definitely a plus to be in the best shape your age and health will allow.

Jeff Chadd: It's extremely important to be fit. Our hunters need to be in the best shape of their life. It's a lot like hunting sheep when you hunt these high-country muleys, and it can ruin a hunt if you're physically unable to do it.

Robb Wiley: The more fit hunters are, the more they can enjoy our part of the country, because it's steep and rugged. I've taken seventy-year-old gentlemen who were seriously overweight, and I've killed some great bucks with some of them because they wouldn't give up. I've also taken some triathlon athletes, guys in the best physical shape possible, and yet they couldn't do what we needed to get a specific deer. Physical fitness isn't a requirement, and there are other,

A patient hunter can accumulate quite a collection of impressive muley bucks. (Photo courtesy Doug Gardner)

more important factors, but it surely does contribute to the enjoyment of the hunt.

Keith Atcheson: Mule deer are found throughout a great swath of western and central North America, and the hunting varies from easy plains hunting in eastern and central Montana to challenging mountain hunts in the Rocky Mountains and southeastern British Columbia. Early season hunts in September are pack-in wilderness hunts, or even backpack affairs, and they require extremely good physical conditioning. Other hunts, such as private land hunts in eastern Montana and Wyoming, are very easy. The hunting can all be easily done on foot and from four-wheel drives. A good and honest outfitter or a reliable hunting consultant can help guide a hunter to the right area. It takes skill to match all the factors for a given hunter, including the hunter's physical ability, experience, and expectations.

Doug Gardner: Good conditioning surely doesn't hurt. If hunters are physically fit, they're better able to take advantage of opportunities as they present. It's not a requirement, by any means, but it's a definite plus. Sometimes we have to get there in a hurry, and it helps if the client can come along at a good pace. It does us no good whatsoever to get there if the client is unable to make it. I've had guides make it to the top of the hill and tell the client as he arrives, out of breath: "He was right there! I wish you'd been here."

That doesn't do anybody any good. I tell my guides not to come back to camp and brag they were able to outwalk their client. That isn't what guiding is about. It's about getting your client in position to take advantage of an opportunity, whatever the client's physical condition.

Fred Lamphere: We do have some rugged country, but we've taken out some men in their eighties, even some who have had hip replacements. They can hunt this rugged country if the guide shifts gears a little and slows down to their pace. It's about taking your time and applying that patience I mentioned. Mule deer are nomadic, and taking the time to glass extensively is very important. Often it's when you're just sitting and glassing that you see the big one. We just watch until he beds, and since we don't hunt areas with a lot of hunting pressure, that animal is bedded for the day. Then we have plenty of time to get over there, no matter what kind of shape the hunter is in.

Thomas Brunson: It really depends on the hunter's expectations. A lot of the areas where we hunt have pretty good road systems, and if the hunter isn't looking for a truly outstanding buck, say 180 or better, then we can usually find a good, mature, representative 5x5, probably 26 to 27 inches wide, fairly close to the road. The more physically fit the hunter, the better chance there is of harvesting a trophy-class animal. We've got a wide variety of habitats here to accommodate all levels of ability. For example, one of the areas we hunt is over eleven thousand feet in elevation, and we hunt it by backpacking. Other units are more rolling piñon-juniper country where it isn't quite as crucial to be physically fit. Overall, though, it's pretty important to be in the best shape you can. If I were going to spend significant money to come on a guided mule deer hunt, I'd sure get in shape for it to the best of my ability.

Ask the Mule Deer Guides

Troy Justensen: It's not all that important in a lot of the units we hunt, but it definitely helps. When you get into some of the high alpine areas, it's extremely important that the hunter be able to get around well in order to have a good chance of success. Basically, it depends on the unit we're hunting.

Jess Rankin: Our mule deer hunting isn't particularly demanding physically in most of our areas, though some of the draw areas we hunt are as difficult as anywhere. There you could wind up doing a lot of walking and glassing. In the Texas Panhandle, almost every buck we kill we spot from the truck.

Bowen Dolhan: Being physically fit isn't the most important factor for our mule deer hunters, but it certainly increases their odds of success. If hunters are fit, I can do about 50 percent more with them in terms of looking over the country and getting to the deer when we find it. Physical fitness doesn't guarantee a trophy, of course, and I've had a lot of out-of-shape people get trophies. It just gives you the ability to take advantage of more opportunities that come your way.

Harry Leuenberger: It's very important because of the way we have to hunt here in the Kootenays. If you spot a big buck up high, you have to be physically fit to get to it. You can't always get horses up to where you need to be, so your own two legs are the only way to approach the animal. Let's just say that your chances of success go up dramatically if you're physically fit.

Nick Frederick: Hunting in Alberta does not require deer hunters to be track stars. Most of the walking is easy, and the vehicle is usually not far away. Pastures and grain fields can be crossed in the vehicle, and sometimes stalks can begin from the truck after the deer is spotted. That keeps the need for great physical stamina to a minimum.

Mick Chapel: It's pretty important, although it depends on the hunt. In Mexico we do a lot of hunting from a high rack in the back of a truck, and physical fitness isn't an issue. Some people don't think it's a very ethical way to hunt, but in some areas it's the only way, and it's very suited to someone who's old, handicapped, overweight, or badly out of shape. It can still be an enjoyable and successful experience for them.

Eduardo Gomez Jr.: Physical conditioning is not so important in most instances, though sometimes it is certainly helpful. If a person is not in shape we try to do the hunt walking slowly, or by trying to get the animal from high towers near water holes or by glassing from a hill.

David Lopez: It is very important because of the long distances we must walk in order to be successful.

How do you handle the inexperienced hunter? The physically challenged hunter?

Grant Adkisson: It takes a lot of patience and a lot of time to deal with either type of hunter. Probably the most inexperienced hunter I ever had was a young man whose uncle had brought him on a hunt. He told me that he had been raised in the city by a single mother and that she wouldn't let him have even a toy gun. As a result he'd never held a gun of any description in his hands. Most inexperienced hunters have at least hunted birds or small game and know a little bit about guns, even if it's only a BB gun. This kid was about thirty years old and had the least experience a person can have. However, he was a willing student and was determined to try. I fitted him with a lightweight rifle we had, and he sat for hours and dry-fired and developed a sight pattern and a good feel for it. When we hunted, I tried to put him in a position not to be rushed to make his shot. The physically challenged hunter takes the same kind of patience, and sometimes some special equipment and setup, such as a blind over a water hole or between bedding and feeding areas. It takes more patience from everybody, but usually both the inexperienced and the physically challenged hunter can be successful.

Jeff Chadd: Inexperienced hunters are no problem if they're in good shape. They listen to you, they learn a lot, and they usually seem to appreciate the hunt. The physically challenged hunter I just can't handle here in Colorado because of the nature of the terrain. We have a big ranch in eastern Montana where we can accommodate physically challenged hunters, but here it's almost impossible.

No matter how you haul him in, this is an awesome buck! (Photo courtesy Fred Lamphere)

Robb Wiley: We often use horses for the physically challenged. We take them to where they approach the end of their comfort level. Sometimes we get creative, perhaps with a deer we've patterned and we know moves through at a particular time of day. Then we'll set the hunter up on it. You've got to be even more patient than usual with the physically challenged, but still you've got to let them do as much as they can without endangering them, and make sure they have a good time. Inexperienced hunters also take a lot of patience, and you've got to walk them through the basics, just as if you were a football coach. You have to explain how to set up the rifle, how to shoot off a backpack, how to use shooting sticks, and be very detailed in your explanations of how everything works. I like to explain to them what we'll do when we see the deer, so they aren't surprised when the moment arrives.

Keith Atcheson: I tend to handle inexperienced hunters by stepping up my level of communication. I want them to understand the decisions we make each day in the field in order to help them become better hunters. I really enjoy working with inexperienced hunters because it's new and exciting to both hunter and guide. I love seeing the excitement on the face of new hunters who take their first game. The best inexperienced hunters I have guided, without a doubt, are women and youngsters. The worst have usually been older professionals who have dedicated little or no time to firearm safety or physical conditioning, and have little respect for or knowledge of the animals they are pursuing. As for physically challenged hunters, I think there is plenty of hunting available for those who cannot get around well. A good outfitter or hunting consultant will direct physically challenged hunters into the right area with the right guide. Then it's the guide's job to accommodate them and help them be comfortable, as well as to get them good opportunities at the species they are pursuing.

Doug Gardner: That's one of our goals here, to mentor the inexperienced hunter, and we get a lot of them. You handle inexperience with communication. The biggest mistake a new hunter can make is to listen to our past clients or their friends who have hunted here with us. What they are often told by them is not to shoot the first deer they see. That may be true most of the time, but they need to be prepared mentally to take advantage of the opportunity to take a good deer when it presents. If that happens to be the very first day and they're not prepared, they can miss their best opportunity of the week. A lot of experience is required for glassing, identifying, judging an animal, and maybe judging distances. That's where a guide comes in, because those are the primary areas he can be of help. They need to trust their guide, and if the opportunity comes early and they elect not to shoot, we let them be the final judge, but we make it clear that they may not find another animal as good. There's also another decision we let hunters make, and that's when they get excited and want to shoot a mediocre deer early in the hunt. If they insist we let them shoot, but we tell them it's a pretty common deer and we're likely to see better. I've seen hunters be very disappointed in themselves as the week progresses and they see much bigger deer coming in. But they've got to be a big enough boy to make a decision and stick by it, or else we really don't want them around.

Physically challenged hunters are limited in mobility, and they appreciate the opportunities we afford them. We tell them that as long as they're able to accept their limitations, we certainly are willing to do everything we can to make them successful. In our style of hunting, it's usually not too hard to get them several opportunities at a nice, representative mule deer. It requires a special permit to shoot from a vehicle in Montana, but if they need it we can get the paperwork for them.

Fred Lamphere: We have quite a number in both categories. With the inexperienced hunter, I like to educate them as we go. For the physically challenged, I look at it as an adventure in overcoming physical obstacles. We've had people in wheelchairs and people who had to use walkers to get around, and they've generally been successful and have had quality hunts. You just have to realize what you've got to help them overcome and then do it.

Thomas Brunson: It takes a huge amount of patience. For inexperienced hunters, I try to feel them out as to their goal for the hunt, and I try to teach them as much as I can. For physically challenged hunters it's all about patience for everybody, and you've got to make them understand that. The hunter and the guide just have to hang in there with whatever setup you've devised and wait until it happens.

Troy Justensen: With inexperienced hunters, it's important to lead them every step of the way and not let them get sidetracked or "hyped" out. I try not to get them either too excited or too low, and just help them get through the hunt in enjoyable fashion. If they miss a buck, I stay positive and let them know we'll find another tomorrow or the next day. Physically challenged hunters are totally different, and guiding them depends entirely on what kind of individual limitation they have. You have to take the hand you're dealt and do the best you can. If a person is confined to a wheelchair, we get a special permit to shoot from the truck and we modify our equipment as needed. The upside is the extreme reward in seeing hunters like that take the mule deer buck of their dreams.

Jess Rankin: I take a lot of disabled hunters in wheelchairs, and they're mostly successful. For both categories, I push the

This hunter followed Grant Adkisson's instructions and was rewarded with this great trophy. (Photo courtesy Grant Adkisson)

Texas hunt a little, because it isn't physically demanding and we can get them set up to shoot from a high seat with a good rest. It's a highly successful hunt for trophy deer, and that way they don't go home with a bad feeling and no deer. If a first-time novice is in really good shape, I'll usually suggest a less expensive but more demanding hunt here in New Mexico, where there's a chance to kill a really big buck, even though the average is just a respectable buck. A few years ago we had two couples hunt with us, and neither wife had ever been hunting before. One of the wives killed a buck that grossed something like 188, and she said, "I don't see what the big deal is about this. All you do is hike around, see one, and shoot him!" I really don't get many novices, though, because we attract mostly experienced hunters.

Ask the Mule Deer Guides

Bowen Dolhan: I've had more inexperienced hunters than I can count, and I've had very few problems with them. I'd take inexperienced hunters anytime. It's just a matter of walking them through all the steps, talking to them about what we're doing, and keeping them informed as to what's going on. I try hard not to give them an information overload, either, because they're learning, and it's better to learn as you go. If I were to start putting in more information than they need or can handle, I'd risk discouraging them. What you do with physically challenged hunters depends on the kind of disability they have. There are a number of ways to handle people who can't get around, such as blinds in a likely spot, but they've got to realize that they're at a disadvantage no matter how we do it. Physically challenged hunters need to go hunting with a very patient mindset. As a guide you assess the degree of physical disability, and then try to make the most of whatever ability they have.

Harry Leuenberger: Inexperience is not a real problem, because most hunters have some degree of it, at least for the area they're hunting. You just talk to them a lot and work with what you've got. The most important experience is that of the guide, so we do quite well with inexperienced hunters. Sometimes you aren't given a choice when it comes to the physically challenged because they just show up and you've got to deal with it. If a person is grossly overweight I might try using a pickup or a quad, but I've had some hunters so heavy I wouldn't put them on one of my horses. When it comes to truly disabled hunters, we just can't deal with them here. The country and the terrain won't let us get a person around adequately in a wheelchair, so it's just impossible.

Nick Frederick: With regard to inexperienced hunters, I ensure that I am with them at all times. I am also there to advise them on every move they make. If you do that for them at these early stages of the hunt they probably will pick up on the right things and never forget them. Safety is a key factor to teach. But everyone needs to start somewhere. Educating hunters at this time in their hunting career has considerable effect on their later experiences, so you must be thorough in your directions and emphasize safety at all times.

Mick Chapel: I've got one guy who's confined to a wheelchair, but he's killed two mule deer bucks over 190, as well as some huge elk and a Boone and Crockett antelope. He's one of those guys I wouldn't want shooting at me, because he gets the job done if he gets an animal in his scope. Inexperienced hunters are usually easy to deal with, because they uniformly listen to what you tell them. When I say, "Shoot him, he's a big one!" they don't ask, "Are you sure?" They just line up and shoot. With some of these prima donna hunters who want to question my judgment, I can usually tell them, "Well, now we don't have to worry about whether it was a big one or not, because he just left!" Those big deer don't stand there very long and give you all the time in the world. And you can forget about coming back tomorrow and finding it standing there again. Give me an inexperienced hunter every time over somebody like that.

Eduardo Gomez Jr.: I think both kinds are the easiest hunters to handle because you explain to them all of the possibilities and they follow the rules much better than most other hunters. They're usually glad just to be there in camp.

David Lopez: The inexperienced hunter is not a problem, because I have a tremendous amount of patience. Also, the inexperienced hunter will usually listen to my instructions better than more experienced hunters. Disabled hunters are more of a problem, depending on the kind of disability they have.

What type of hunter do you most dislike guiding? Is there any particular characteristic that would make you refuse to guide a hunter?

Grant Adkisson: I've already mentioned my dislike for guiding the unappreciative hunter. I'd add to that the hunter who refuses to listen to anything the guide or outfitter has to say. There are hunters who think they already know it all, so they don't have to listen to the guide or respect the guide's experience. I don't think I've ever refused to guide a hunter, but if I knew ahead of time that a person was completely unteachable, I very well might refuse.

Ask the Mule Deer Guides

Jeff Chadd: This one could get me in trouble! The hunters I most dislike have a big head and a big ego and think they know it all. Maybe they've hunted Dall sheep and grizzly, and after one day of mule deer hunting they've got it down pat and know more than I do. As far as refusing to let a hunter come back, it would have to be some kind of safety issue, such as leaving a shell in the chamber after I've said to take it out.

Robb Wiley: I don't like a bad attitude, which is usually manifested by expecting too much and being unwilling to put out the necessary effort. A bad attitude in camp can spoil everyone else's attitude, too. There are definitely a few hunters we've had who might telephone and discover that we're booked for the foreseeable future. Most of the time it's because they don't respect the animal we're hunting, and they don't respect the time and effort that's been put into giving them a good opportunity. We do an incredible amount of preseason scouting, and we do the very best we can for every client every time. Despite that, we have some clients come in with expectations of killing a 200-inch mule deer or nothing, and they don't respect anything that falls short. They seem to view the hunt as a glory thing for themselves. They don't care how much effort has been put into their hunt or that there are some great mule deer that won't score well.

Keith Atcheson: The type of hunter I most dislike guiding is the one that simply kills animals for the thrill of it and has no respect for the animal's life or the meat. I also particularly dislike guiding hunters who are repeatedly warned about firearms safety and seem to ignore it. The type of hunter I would refuse to guide is the loud, arrogant, obnoxious, aggressive sort that drinks to excess and is dangerous with firearms. I have fired more than one client in my guiding career, and outfitters and guides should know that it is OK to do that when necessary. Get rid of the problem early and fast. You will not regret it, even if you have to refund their money. Other items on my "DO NOT DO" list would be discharging firearms in hunting camp, accidentally or otherwise; making a decision to shoot an animal that turns out to be smaller than expected and then blaming the guide or

Age doesn't matter when the hunter follows instructions well. (Photo courtesy Keith Atcheson)

outfitter; not following the suggested equipment list or payment schedule; misrepresenting one's physical abilities; and making unwanted sexual advances toward women in camp.

Doug Gardner: I've never seen a hunter I'd refuse to guide, but there have certainly been hunters that I'd refuse to have back a second time. There are a couple of characteristics that really stick out. One is the person who desperately wants a trophy deer but lacks the patience to be a trophy deer hunter. The other is the person who's so full of himself that he refuses to admit he has any limitations. A common example is shooting ability. A hunter like that who misses an animal will blame the guide for misjudging the distance or claim that there's something wrong with the rifle. Well, people miss mostly because they're excited. It's normal for your heart to be going an extra beat or two when you're shooting at an animal, otherwise why are you hunting? But that type of guy just can't admit it. I've also had some who couldn't distinguish between having a drink in camp or on the way back after the hunt, and drinking in the middle of the day while they're hunting. I don't have much use for someone who can't make that distinction.

Fred Lamphere: I don't like to guide hunters who are in a big hurry. They come out knowing exactly what they want, and they want it now. Sometimes they want a 180-class deer and nothing less, and they may have booked a five-day hunt but can stay only three. They still want that 180 buck, and they want me to put them on it. We get some like that every year. I know that a lot of people are so busy they don't have a lot of time to savor the hunt, because they've got so many irons in the fire. They sure add a different twist to a hunt. As far as refusing to guide a hunter, I've never refused a hunter, at least not the first time around. If we have a personality clash or if the hunter has some habits that I can't abide, I might refuse the second time. There really isn't anything I can bring to mind that would make me turn down a hunter to start with. If a hunter does something unethical on the hunt, I'd refuse to guide them a second time. You know, I probably have a bit of an advantage in the ethics department because, in addition to guiding, I'm the sheriff of

Butte County, South Dakota. Inasmuch as I'm a law enforcement officer and also a hunter safety instructor, nobody is going to offer me a bribe to overlook a game law violation or try to pay me to let them dump an animal they think is too small so they can look for something better. Most of my clients are above that kind of thing, anyway.

Thomas Brunson: As I said before, the know-it-all hunters are my pet peeve. I'm a pretty easygoing guy, though, and I'd never refuse to guide a hunter unless he demonstrates that he is completely unsafe with the weapon.

Troy Justensen: I don't know if I can pinpoint it to just one thing. Of all the hunters I've guided, there are probably no more than one or two I'd refuse to guide again. The reason in those cases is their total disrespect for the animal based on what it tapes. Usually the animal measures very close to what we say it will, but if it's even a quarter-inch short of their expectations a hunter like that comes unglued and blames everybody but himself. There's one guy I'm thinking about in that regard. I told him that the deer would go over 30 inches wide and he shot it. When we walked up to it, he said, "This deer won't go over 21." I told him it would be exactly what I had said, a good 30 inches. I don't usually carry a tape on me, so we had to wait until we were back in camp to do a measurement, which was done by another guide and showed the deer at 32. The guy still wasn't satisfied! To each his own, I guess, but I wouldn't subject myself to a guy like that again, knowing what I now know about him.

Jess Rankin: The only reason I've ever refused a hunter is because he's a bad drinker in camp. I've seldom told a hunter on the phone that I won't take him, though I have had a couple of guys I didn't book because they started doing price comparisons to a high-fence operation, when there was no comparison in the hunt experience. I just won't take someone who doesn't appreciate the difference between a high-fence hunt and a free-range hunt.

Bowen Dolhan: I really don't like the negative, pessimistic attitude I mentioned earlier. As far as my refusing to guide a hunter on an initial hunt, there have been very few. Those have

Ask the Mule Deer Guides

been the ones who had expectations that were unrealistic and who wanted more than I could reasonably deliver. Most of them wanted a 200-inch deer virtually guaranteed. Sure, we kill that kind of deer every year, but if that seems to be the hunter's expectation, I keep away. If I perceive that the 200 mark is the most important thing about the hunt to that hunter, I would refuse to guide.

Harry Leuenberger: I don't like an overly aggressive person or an arrogant person. Unfortunately, you don't know about someone until you're out in the field. You can tell a little about people by talking to them on the phone, but we get some through booking agents that we've not had the opportunity to talk to. I wouldn't have someone back for a second time who is so out of shape that our style of hunting is impossible. I just tell them the truth.

Nick Frederick: I most dislike guiding a hunter that fails to communicate with me. It's really not fair when a hunter saves a complaint until he returns home and then tells everyone except the guide or outfitter that there was a problem. There is a saying: If you're happy with our service, tell others. If you're not, tell us. Ninety-five percent of problems that occur on a hunt can be resolved before the hunt ends if they are brought out into the open and discussed. The exact opposite is true if you hold on to the problems until you get home and then try to resolve them. Communication is the key, whether with your guide or with the outfitter himself. It's also difficult to guide a hunter with a negative outlook. Both guide and hunter must keep a positive attitude while trophy hunting. It's extremely difficult to guide a hunter who appears to have no faith in you as a guide.

Mick Chapel: A guy who's got no money! No, I'm kidding! It's the know-it-all type who's always questioning everything the guide does. Are you sure there are deer here? Why don't I see any? Why haven't we seen any all morning? Then, when they get back to camp, they start questioning the other hunters. Seen any deer? How much did you pay for your hunt? They're just trying to stir up trouble. Maybe it's hot and there's a full moon and you're going to have to hunt hard to find the big ones.

All kinds of things affect the hunting, even barometric pressure, humidity, and dew point, and we may not even be aware of them. But a know-it-all hunter isn't aware of that, and he's just so full of drivel that it drives me nuts!

Eduardo Gomez Jr.: Hunters who lack experience yet believe they know everything about hunting mule deer. They've read all the magazine articles and that makes them an expert.

David Lopez: The kind of hunter I do not like to guide is one who is out of shape and has little or no patience. I am not able to do a good job of guiding someone who cannot walk well.

What is the worst thing a client can do on a hunt?

Grant Adkisson: The worst thing is not being safe. If you put your guide, yourself, or others in danger by shooting at a sound or handling a firearm in an unsafe manner, that's just plain stupid. When we talk to clients we stress getting ready for the hunt by practicing and by doing some shooting from unusual positions, but we always emphasize having a safe hunt. The first night in camp we go over some of that as well, because even some experienced hunters are safe when hunting alone but are not used to following along behind a guide. They have to learn what's safe for the guide, too. The main thing is watching which way the gun is pointed.

Jeff Chadd: The worst is when they come ill prepared, unable to fire their rifle, maybe haven't sighted in their rifle, don't have good gear such as footwear, and are out of shape.

Robb Wiley: I'd say the worst thing would be to give up. Hunting mule deer with success is 99 percent mental, and when somebody gives up mentally, they might as well go home.

Keith Atcheson: I would rank being unsafe with firearms as the worst thing a hunter can do. One of the greatest sources of simple irritation is when a client arrives, pulls out a wad of cash, and tries to bribe the guide into producing a large trophy animal, as if that were possible. That sort of thing may be an incentive to some guides, but most take great pride in their work and always do the best they can whatever the payoff. Besides, any

Would the big boy in the middle give you buck fever? (Photo courtesy Nick Frederick)

good guide knows that no amount of money is going to produce an animal that might not even exist.

Doug Gardner: I think the worst is to harvest a deer and then be totally dissatisfied with it. That gives me a sick feeling. We try to give good advice and tell hunters what kind of deer it is, but whether they shoot the wrong animal or we make a bad call, if they wind up unhappy with the result it's really disappointing to me.

Fred Lamphere: The worst thing they can do is be disrespectful of the game animal or of other people in camp. In our camps we've had a little bit of that, but it hasn't really been much of an issue.

Thomas Brunson: I don't know if it's the very worst thing they can do, but it really bugs me when hunters show up without sighting in their rifle or with improper footwear that causes blisters right off the bat. I've had both those things happen.

Troy Justensen: I think the worst is losing enthusiasm and developing a bad attitude. There are certain things on a hunt that I can control, but there are far more that I can't. That's why we call it hunting and not killing. It's especially the case when you're looking for a real trophy mule deer, because often it takes a lot of time, effort, and patience. When things aren't going exactly to suit you, you've got to keep a positive attitude and just keep on hunting expectantly.

Jess Rankin: Drinking while hunting or excessive drinking in camp both come to mind. Also, if a hunter isn't safe with a firearm, that's pretty bad. The two problems seem to run hand in hand, by the way.

Bowen Dolhan: Shoot himself or the guide! That's a pretty broad question, though, so I'll narrow it down a little. Anytime there's a problem, it needs to be addressed, not kept quiet. I say this to get around to the need for communication. If there's any problem with the hunt, talk to the guide or talk to the outfitter. Let him know in a nice way that there's a problem, because nobody can fix anything without first knowing there's a problem. That's what we've always told our clients. Another problem I'd mention is when the hunter constantly doubts the guide. Lack of confidence in a guide really throws him off so that he can't perform up to full potential.

Harry Leuenberger: I've had hunters who have handled firearms in an unsafe manner, and I think that's the worst because they're putting human life at risk.

Nick Frederick: One of the worst things a hunter can do on a trip is talk about the Boone and Crockett Club in every sentence. In my opinion, measuring tapes have ruined more hunts than any other single factor.

Mick Chapel: Miss the big one! That happens so much you just can't believe it. It's a shame, because it's not just the hunter who gets hurt. It really lets the guide down, too. Every guide wants to pull into camp with the big one in the back of the truck, and the hunter who can't shoot straight has ruined that opportunity even though the guide did his job perfectly. We do elk hunts, too, and missing has become so bad that I've put a limit on it. If a hunter wounds two elk, he's done. Before I put that policy into place, I had one guy wound eleven bulls on an archery elk hunt before he killed one. We don't let that happen anymore. I've even had hunters come in and wound three or four and then go home mad because they didn't get one! Now, after two incidents of drawing blood, they're done. They need to go home and practice some more.

Eduardo Gomez Jr.: Safety is the most important part of any hunt, and unsafe handling of firearms is the worst thing a hunter can do. It can cost a life, in fact.

David Lopez: The worst thing is when they can't move around without making too much noise. We are hunting a very spooky animal, and if we can't move around quietly we may never see the deer we're hunting, no matter how hard we try.

Chapter 4

MULE DEER GUIDES EVALUATE HUNTING ARMS

What is your favorite rifle caliber for mule deer?

Grant Adkisson: My father always used a .270, and he had one in pre-'64 Winchester. My first gun for deer was a 1903 Springfield .30-06, because it was cheap. I switched over to a .270 later on, and I've used a lot of different rifles since. I encourage hunters to use the caliber they're most comfortable with and that they shoot best.

Jeff Chadd: That's a tough question. You need a flat-shooting rifle, for sure. The 7mm STW (Shooting Times Western) is one of the best, in my opinion. It's a wildcat cartridge that was made by Remington for a while, but nobody is making them now. But I'll tell you what, if you use 160-grain bullets and get it sighted in right, you can hold dead on out to four hundred yards and it will do the job. The new short magnums are also excellent.

Robb Wiley: I really like the Remington .300 Ultramag. It has plenty of reach and plenty of knockdown power. We have some really long shots out here at times, up to four hundred yards, and a rifle like that has plenty of power to do the job downrange.

Keith Atcheson: Without a doubt, my favorite rifle caliber for mule deer is a .30-06. We have had well over a thousand clients in our mule deer and antelope hunting camps over the years, and we have seen every possible caliber come through. There is no question in my mind that the .270 and .30-06 are the best all-round calibers. All things considered, the .30-06 is the most versatile, well-rounded caliber in North America. I choose the .30-06 as my own weapon for pronghorn antelope, white-tailed deer, mule deer, and many other species worldwide. It has such an incredible range of bullet weights that you can use it for nearly all applications. Simply put, the .30-06 works!

A great Sonora buck taken with a modern firearm. (Photo courtesy Eduardo Gomez)

Doug Gardner: My personal favorite is the 7mm Winchester Magnum because I'm comfortable with it and I don't have to worry about the distance until it's beyond three hundred yards. I tell all my hunters that topping the rifle with good optics is more important than the rifle's make, model, or caliber.

Fred Lamphere: Personally, I like a .25-06. I've had one since I was twenty years old. My brother-in-law had one before that, and I was always borrowing it. I like the caliber because it's a flat-shooting rifle with plenty of speed and versatility. Some might argue that it's a little light, but I'm comfortable shooting it and I'll argue shot placement over caliber all day long.

Thomas Brunson: I've seen a lot of people take good mule deer with a .243, and anything from that on up is an adequate caliber. My personal favorite is the Remington 7mm Ultramag because it's fast and flat-shooting, and the majority of our shots are between three and five hundred yards. With that rifle you have to use a bullet that holds together well, like the Barnes Triple-Shock, because the speed is problematic for some bullets.

Troy Justensen: I'm a wildcat fanatic, so any of the fast wildcats are my favorites. For factory rifles, I really like Remington's .300 Ultramag. I use 180-grain Barnes X-Bullets in it.

Jess Rankin: I've got a .264 Winchester Magnum that shoots really flat and straight. I love the rifle. It's my favorite for all big game.

Bowen Dolhan: My favorite is the .300 Winchester Magnum.

Harry Leuenberger: I've always used a 7mm Winchester Magnum. I also have a .243 that I sometimes carry.

Nick Frederick: I'm not heavily into calibers, so I don't really have a personal favorite.

Mick Chapel: I love the .300 Winchester Magnum. It's the best big-game rifle for the Western United States.

Eduardo Gomez Jr.: My personal favorite is the .300 Winchester Magnum. It has all the best characteristics for taking a desert mule deer.

David Lopez: I like the .30-06 better than any other.

What caliber do you recommend for clients?

Grant Adkisson: Many clients have the idea that they need a big magnum to shoot flat enough to take a mule deer. Those guns are very effective for hunters who can shoot them well. However, the average hunter can become afraid of the recoil and doesn't really like shooting them. Such a hunter would be much better off with a .270 or a .30-06 than a big magnum. There's also a difference being on a paid hunt with a guide and hunting on your own in your local area. A guy can be very accurate and select his shots at home and never regret using a .243. He may have a .30-06 he shoots equally well, but he simply prefers the .243 for some reason. I'd encourage him to bring the .30-06, if he's equally comfortable with it, because on a five-day guided hunt there may be no choice but to take a less than perfect shot. The little bit of extra bullet weight might make the difference between killing that buck and wounding and losing it.

Jeff Chadd: I tell hunters to bring something they're comfortable shooting, whether it's a .270 or whatever. I personally don't like the .30-06, but it's OK if that's their choice.

Ask the Mule Deer Guides

Robb Wiley: I like a .30 caliber. More important than the caliber, though, is preparing the shot ahead of time so it can be placed accurately. It doesn't take a big gun to do the job. A .30 caliber allows one to be just a little less accurate and still do enough damage that we can catch up to the deer. I really hate more than almost anything wounding and losing an animal, and a larger caliber helps prevent that.

Keith Atcheson: As I said before, either a .270 or a .30-06 would be my choice, all other factors being equal.

Doug Gardner: I recommend that clients bring the rifle they shoot most accurately. I really don't have a particular caliber to recommend, because bullet placement is so much more important than any other factor. A very light caliber that they can shoot accurately does have limitations in high wind and at long range, but a big, powerful gun they can't shoot well is no use under any conditions.

Fred Lamphere: I'd recommend any caliber they're comfortable shooting, down to the .243. I don't like seeing anything smaller than that. That being said, I'd still rather have someone come out with even a .223 they can use to drive tacks out to 250 yards than a brand-new .300 magnum that just kicked the crap out of them at the range. With that new rifle, they aren't comfortable and they aren't competent.

Thomas Brunson: I tell them to use anything that shoots flat, from the .25-06 on up to the .30 calibers. Some guys will bring the big .300 magnums, but most people can't shoot those as accurately as they can a .243.

Troy Justensen: Any .30-caliber rifle is hard to beat. Anything in the .300 Winchester, .300 Ultramag, or any other of the .30 calibers is acceptable. I'm not nearly as concerned with caliber, though, as I am with their ability to shoot the gun and not be afraid of it. They've got to be accurate and not flinch when they shoot. Bullet placement is the prime factor, no matter what caliber a hunter is packing, and I'd rather see hunters toting a .243 they can shoot accurately. If they're afraid to pull the trigger, you won't have to worry about bullet placement, because they'll probably miss the whole animal.

Mule Deer Guides Evaluate Hunting Arms

Jess Rankin: A .270 is a really good mule deer gun. Some of the new short magnums are flat-shooting, too, and I'd recommend them if a guy asks. The main thing about the caliber is that the hunter needs to be familiar and comfortable with it. I've taken a lot of kids hunting for both elk and mule deer, and I'd far prefer they be comfortable shooting a .243 than be carrying a bigger rifle they're afraid to fire.

Bowen Dolhan: I like the 7mm magnums, the .300 magnums, or even the .338, because they pack a good punch. I like the heavier guns because our mule deer here in Alberta weigh between three and four hundred pounds. We also have a lot of really ugly places, brushy creeks and their drainages, where wounded bucks can run and never be found. The bigger guns put them down as quickly as possible with the best margin for error. If the shot is poorly placed, an animal can run a lot longer if it's hit with a .270 than if it's hit with a .300 magnum, because the .300 does a lot of damage even if it doesn't hit the vitals.

Harry Leuenberger: I'd say to pick a flat-shooting rifle with which they're really comfortable. They need as much reach as possible, but they need to be able to shoot the gun without flinching.

Nick Frederick: I personally do not put much emphasis on calibers. I find it best to trust the experience a hunter has with his gun, regardless of the caliber. I've had hunters for mule deer with many calibers from .243 all the way up to the .375 Winchester Magnum. One of my hunters used a .375, and he was as knowledgeable about ballistics and guns as any hunter I have ever known. He took both his mule deer and his whitetail with one-shot kills. He put the bullet right through vital areas, and to my surprise bullet damage showed that his choice of weapon was not overkill. Another hunter I guided for many years was adamant about using his little .243. Every buck he shot died within a minute or less, even the ones pushing three hundred pounds. So the bottom line is this: Hit them right, and most calibers are just fine for mule deer. Still, these are very big deer up here, and I would recommend that you shoot the biggest caliber you can handle comfortably.

Ask the Mule Deer Guides

Mick Chapel: I don't necessarily recommend a .300 Winchester Magnum for everybody, even though I said it's my personal favorite. Hunters should shoot the gun they're most at ease with. They don't need to bring too much gun. If they do, they're shell-shocked and can't shoot straight. They know they're going to get kicked badly, and they just can't get the job done. Never let a young person shoot a gun like that, or he'll be shell-shocked for the rest of his life. I'd rather hunters carry a .243 than a cannon they can't handle.

Eduardo Gomez Jr.: If the client can handle the recoil and shoot it accurately, I'd stick with the .300 Winchester Magnum. If not, I'd ask them to bring whatever rifle they shoot most accurately and comfortably.

David Lopez: I'd recommend the .300 Weatherby Magnum, if the hunter can shoot it well. If it's too much gun, then bring what you shoot best.

What is your advice on bullet weight? Bullet construction?

Grant Adkisson: I like a well-constructed bullet like a Nosler Partition. That's where you should start and work your way out from there. A bullet should pattern well in the gun you're going to use, and it should be of a type that retains its weight well. For weight I'm in the middle, so for a .270 it's the 130-grain; for the .30-06 something around 150–165 grains, and for most calibers I'd recommend using something that's not the heaviest or the lightest bullet available. You've got to experiment a little, too, to find the one that shoots best in your particular rifle, and that takes a lot of work at the shooting range.

Jeff Chadd: I like a medium-weight bullet, something like 150–160 grains. I really like the Nosler Partitions, if they pattern well in the hunter's rifle.

Robb Wiley: I love a 180-grain Scirocco. That is the bullet I use myself. It's somewhat similar to a ballistic tip, being something of a cross between a ballistic tip and a partition bullet. It flies like a ballistic tip and holds together like a Nosler Partition, which is a good combination.

In some areas muzzleloader season is a great time to hunt. (Photo courtesy Troy Justensen)

Ask the Mule Deer Guides

Keith Atcheson: I feel that the best bullet weight to use on mule deer is 150–180 grains. My favorite bullets include the Nosler Partition, Swift A-Frames, and Barnes Triple-Shock X-Bullets. The worst bullets ever made for hunting are the ballistic tip, and I refuse to let a client use them if I can help it. We have had more wounded game and problems from that bullet failing than from any other bullet by far. At all costs, stay away from them.

Doug Gardner: You want a bullet that expands when it hits the heart-lung area. If hunters are going to do what I've always done and hold on the shoulder, I don't think you can beat Nosler Partitions or something similar.

Fred Lamphere: I like a good bonded bullet that will hold together on impact. Muleys are tough, and if the bullet comes apart on entering the body you don't get good penetration and can wind up with a bad result. I like the heaviest bullet the rifle shoots accurately.

Thomas Brunson: I'm a big fan of bonded core bullets and any of the sturdier bullets that hold together well. In a .270 the Nosler Partition bullets do great, but in a faster, flatter-shooting rifle they don't pattern well and I prefer the Barnes concept.

Troy Justensen: I really like the Barnes X-Bullet. I also like Nosler Partition bullets, and any good ballistic-tip bullet. I'm personal friends with Randy Brooks, and I like his bullets. They perform well, and I'd certainly recommend them as top of the line.

Jess Rankin: For mule deer you don't really need the most weight-retaining bullet in the world. I like the 140-grain Swift Scirocco in .264 or 7mm.

Bowen Dolhan: I'm a fan of the 180-grain Nosler Partitions or Nosler AccuBond bullets.

Harry Leuenberger: Bullet weight depends entirely on the caliber. In a .243, 100 grains is the ticket, and in a 7mm it's a 140-grain bullet. As for construction, I'd again tell hunters to pick one that performs well in their particular rifle. Deer aren't incredibly hard to kill, anyway—it's not like shooting a Cape buffalo! Bullet placement will tell the tale more than caliber almost every time.

Nick Frederick: As I indicated earlier, I'm not much into the bullet style and weight debate. I let the hunters decide what they are most comfortable using, keeping in mind that we do have very big mule deer bucks in Alberta.

Mick Chapel: I don't have any strong opinions on that, because it's not nearly as important as where you hit the animal. You're going to get a lot of penetration with a .300 Magnum, and wherever you hit the animal we're probably going to recover it.

Eduardo Gomez Jr.: I prefer bullets with soft points that expand in controlled fashion. I'm not an expert on ballistics, but I believe those bullets give the best combination of penetration and bullet integrity.

David Lopez: I know very little about this topic, but it should be a bullet that will definitely kill the deer.

Do you have any tips on shooting techniques in field situations?

Grant Adkisson: I started using a homemade bipod in the late 1960s, not attached to the gun but just two sticks hooked together. I got that from pictures of the old buffalo hunters using such a device for shooting long distances. Shooting sticks are still a favorite of mine and can be a big advantage to the hunter. Practice is a big factor, but too many of our hunters come out without having shot their gun since last season. You just can't be proficient if you don't practice.

Jeff Chadd: I like to tell them to be comfortable to four hundred yards from a number of positions, whether with shooting sticks or whatever. This is the hunt of a lifetime, so they need to be ready.

Robb Wiley: Most people take their rifle to the range and shoot from the bench, but once it's sighted in they give no more thought to preparing to shoot. I do totally recommend sandbags or whatever else you need to sight in the rifle, making sure it's shooting properly and making a very tight group, but you shouldn't stop there. After that you should put the sandbags away, get off the bench, and do some real practice for what you're going to encounter in the field. Practice shooting short

Archery season is a good time to catch bucks in velvet in some areas—and they're significantly less wary at that time of year. (Photo courtesy Bowen Dolhan)

distances, long distances, uphill, downhill, off a backpack, off a rock or tree, and so on. That's really far more important than shooting the gun at the range. I also highly recommend shooting sticks for every hunter.

Keith Atcheson: The best advice I could give to clients is to find a good rest or not shoot at all. Lying down prone with a good rest or over a backpack, sitting on your rear and bracing with your knees, or using a rock or tree to stabilize your weapon are all very effective. Shooting sticks and bipods are great but can be time consuming to set up when the need arises. Good hunters are always looking around or thinking ahead so they can position themselves for the shot. A good hunting guide literally "sees" his client into a shooting position. That can be done by actually taking the rifle ahead and placing it in a resting position, crawling aside, and having the client crawl into the shooting position, or simply explaining to the client what to do. A lot depends on the guide's experience. In final stalks that require crawling on your hands and knees or belly crawling, a guide should always have the client next to him instead of behind him. Rifle safety is of the utmost importance, but it's easy to forget that at the last moment when people are excited. Always have the barrel of the rifle pointing in the other direction and away from people. In some cases I have taken control of the rifle, placed it in shooting position, and had my client crawl up to take the shot. My chances of being hurt are far less when I handle the final stalk like that. It might not be necessary for every client, but there is certainly a place for the technique.

Doug Gardner: I tell my clients that any rest is a good rest. We carry shooting sticks all the time, and we also recommend a bipod. Anytime you can get steady with a solid rest, you're far better off. I'd rather have a client take a shot with a solid rest at a standing deer 250 yards away than jump the animal out of its bed and try an offhand shot at 60 yards. Not only do we have a better chance to judge the deer, but we've also got time to get a good, solid rest.

Fred Lamphere: We visit a lot with our hunters once they book a hunt, and I always recommend they set up a little shooting range using milk jugs with colored water in them. That depends, of course, on where they live and whether they have a good place to shoot. If it's possible, I have them set out the jugs and then shoot at them from various positions. They need to be able to shoot offhand from a hundred yards or so, and they should be able to do it in varying field conditions—windy days, cloudy days, sunny days, whatever. They need to put themselves in a few challenging situations, because there aren't many times we have that buck standing up in front of a shooting bench. They need to know that they can shoot offhand, because a lot of times when you're stalking you're going to bump right into a buck. I've had too many people who have practiced and practiced off the bench, but when it comes to lying down and shooting off the ground, it's entirely new to them. They've never shot from that position, so they shoot over the top of the animal. They just need to do a little practice ahead of time.

Thomas Brunson: I just won't let my hunter shoot unless we've got a dead rest. I'm not talking about a tree limb or a rock

Grant Adkisson hunts with a modern firearm or bow and takes some wonderful Colorado bucks. (Photo courtesy Grant Adkisson)

or shooting sticks. The rifle has to be flat on the ground. As I said, our country is such that most of our shots are very long, so usually we get down in the prone position. I want that rifle as steady as if it were on a shooting bench. Hunters should practice that position, as well as others, just to be sure they can handle it.

Troy Justensen: Knowing your gun and being able to shoot it well in any situation are so very important. I prefer that a hunter shoot off either shooting sticks or a bipod. It's not uncommon in our wide-open country to be shooting between three and four hundred yards. If you're not steady, it's just a long miss.

Jess Rankin: I've got a friend in the outfitting business who books a lot of hunters out of the Harrisburg, Pennsylvania, hunting show every year, and most of them have never had to shoot from anywhere but a bench or a tree stand. They never get the opportunity to shoot at a moving animal, but I grew up shooting at jack rabbits with my .22. Sometimes a mule deer hunt involves doing a drive or jumping a deer, and you've got to be able to hit an animal on the move. I hate for somebody to tell me that they're not comfortable with a shot, and I get really frustrated. If you want comfort, buy a La-Z-Boy. But if you want to kill a big mule deer, you should learn to shoot a running animal. I don't know how to tell an Eastern hunter how to practice making running shots, but they have to figure out a way and then do it.

Bowen Dolhan: Let me cover one for bow hunters and one for rifle hunters. For the bow hunter, always shoot for the spot that gives you the best margin for error. When you're stalking a mule deer that's lying down, you've got to aim for the bottom third of the deer. You should aim just a little bit farther back, instead of trying to tuck the arrow tight into the shoulder. Move back a little and give yourself more margin for error. Try to split the difference between the liver and up tight to the shoulder. Don't aim tight for the shoulder, because you might either hit the leg or skip off the shoulder bone and have a wounded animal that you'll never recover. For rifle hunters, you've just got to be packing a rest with you. Shooting sticks are fine, and there are a couple of different kinds that work well. I really like a tripod

How would you approach this bedded Alberta buck with archery or muzzleloader equipment? (Photo courtesy Nick Frederick)

type of arrangement: three poles held together with an elastic band. That's really stable and a good shooting platform. A bipod is sometimes OK, but they aren't tall enough for our kind of hunting because the vegetation is often more than three feet high. You're always shooting from a standing position here, and our shots average about two hundred yards.

Harry Leuenberger: Get the best rest you can get before shooting. We have a lot of long shots, and 300 to 350 yards isn't at all unreasonable. I need to get the hunter on as solid a dead rest as possible. There are several ways to do that. We often use a pack and shoot from the prone position. Shooting sticks can be a big help, too. The only problem with bipods is that they don't fit well in a rifle scabbard, and we use horses a lot. What I recommend instead is the tripod that we use for our spotting scopes. We can take off the scope and flip the handle over so there's a nice "V" to use as a rifle rest. It works perfectly. You can even set it up on the side of a hill and shoot from a sitting position.

Nick Frederick: The nice thing about mule deer hunting in Alberta is that maybe 80 percent of the time you will be given a standing shot. I always try to get the hunter such an opportunity. If you give the deer room to move in our country and don't push too hard, you can often find it again and try another stalk if the first one doesn't work out. Most of the country in our region provides you with miles of open land mixed with brush and river bottoms. There is always an opening the buck must cross before the next piece of cover. Because of that I sometimes find bucks again and can give the hunter another chance. Most often they don't blow the second one.

Mick Chapel: A bipod is a great asset. You've also got to stay calm, and that's not one of my strong points, unfortunately, because I can get pretty emotional. I'm trying to work on that, because it's so important not to let emotions get in the way. Calm down, evaluate the situation, and make sure everything is right before you shoot, if you've got the time.

Eduardo Gomez Jr.: Shoot as calmly as possible and do not pull the trigger unless you are sure you are going to hit the animal. The hunter should always be well prepared and ready to shoot without delay.

David Lopez: It is very important for the shooter to have a good, solid rest, so his shot is accurate.

How do you prepare for and handle "buck fever" (overpowering excitement) in a client?

Grant Adkisson: I like to communicate with the hunter to try to defuse the situation. It helps to watch hunting videos and the like. A lot of guides and outfitters are a little reluctant to talk to their hunter just before the shot, but I've actually gone the other way. I talk hunters through the shot, especially if they show any sign of buck fever. I've had several guys develop the problem, and I've eased right up beside them and talked them through it. I tell them to take a deep breath and relax, don't worry about it; if we don't get this one we'll find you another. Sometimes I even hold up my hand and demonstrate exactly where to hold the cross hairs on the animal.

A mighty fine Colorado buck taken with a modern firearm. (Photo courtesy Jeff Chadd)

Jeff Chadd: I just slap them up side the head and tell them to sit down! No, I'm kidding! I do everything I can to get them to calm down. I have threatened them if they just refuse to do so, because all they have to do is settle down, take their time, and get off a good shot.

Robb Wiley: A lot depends on the client. There are definitely times when I get excited myself, and we try to hold that back as much as possible, because often when the guide gets excited it really cranks up the person you're guiding. Sometimes it takes some forceful direction—of the sort a football coach might do—

telling the client exactly what to do at every step. Most people don't need that, but if I can tell someone is rattled, I step in.

Keith Atcheson: Buck fever is a fact of life in hunting. I think that one major reason we hunt is for the incredible excitement. We are predators and providers. However, every once in a while buck fever can get the best of us, and once you have it there isn't much you can do about it while it's happening. The best thing a guide can do for a client like that is to talk in a soothing, calming voice and not get excited. If the guide gets excited the client will become even more pumped up, and inevitably everything goes downhill from there. Live and learn from buck fever and try to do better on your next opportunity. Controlling the problem is ultimately in the hands of the shooter, but a calming, direct-speaking guide can sometimes help a hunter to calm down enough to make the shot. Getting unnerved as a guide, shouting at clients to shoot fast, or letting your own emotions run wild all work against everyone's ultimate success.

Doug Gardner: I try to visit with the hunter and explain ahead of time how the hunt might go. I tell hunters I want them to be excited, but I try to let them know there's no pressure. They should realize ahead of time that if we miss an opportunity, we're still hunting and we'll try to find another one. I think that preparation ahead of time is a big key to heading off a bad case of the shakes. I've had experienced trophy hunters who are looking for something really special come unglued on the last day of the hunt when we find an outstanding deer, and you can't do much for that, I'm afraid.

Fred Lamphere: I watch my hunter closely. If I see the hunter start to breathe shallowly and get the shakes, I just put my hand over the scope and call for a break. The thing about our hunts is that the deer aren't hunted hard, and when you're on a guided hunt you're not usually hunting public land, where you have to shoot quickly or someone else might get the buck. A lot of the hunters we get have saved up for a time for this hunt, and it's easy for them to get buck fever. I like to break that as soon as I see it. I know from my law enforcement training and my hunter safety courses that buck fever isn't a lot different from

By whatever weapon it was taken, this is an impressive deer. (Photo courtesy Robb Wiley)

"tunnel vision," which is a kind of trance people get into. You just have to stop, take a few breaths, and break out of that trance. Most hunters really appreciate your helping them through it.

Thomas Brunson: I have them take their time and breathe a little, and I really try not to rush them. If you can get them to relax and take it slow, they don't usually get spooked. The other thing is that I try not to get excited myself, and unless we've already discussed it I don't tell them how big I think the deer might be. Excitement is contagious, so the guide has to play it cool. Every hunter can sense excitement in the guide, and if the guide is excited it can cause the hunter to develop a bad case of buck fever.

Troy Justensen: First of all I try to keep myself under control, and that means keeping the client a little bit in the dark if you're looking at a truly grand old buck. I never mention the score, because numbers like 240 or 250 are bound to start the adrenaline pumping. A huge part of the guide's job is to be able to keep a hunter calm through any situation. It sure helps to have someone behind you who's cool and mellow, because that makes it a lot easier to make the shot. Often I'll intentionally downplay the buck a little. If it's a truly heart-stopping deer and the client asks what the buck will score, I try to put off any such speculation until we have the buck on the ground. I just say, "Make a good shot. You'll like him!"

Jess Rankin: You simply talk the hunter through the situation and keep calm yourself. The worst thing the guide can do is to start yelling at a client because that just gets the hunter more upset—and more likely to shake worse than ever.

Bowen Dolhan: I try not to get excited myself, and I try to calm the hunter down by slowly walking through the steps of what we're going to do. I try to get my hunters to take their time. I make sure the gun is loaded and the client's looking at the right buck. I remind him what kind of distance we're dealing with, where exactly to aim on the animal, and so on. You can usually avoid severe buck fever if you do things that way. I sometimes have a client wait until the animal presents broadside, and I talk to them all the while. If the guy is shaking so badly that the end of the barrel is bouncing like crazy, I don't hesitate to pull the hunter off and pass on the opportunity. That can mean waiting until we can get closer, or even waiting for another day. I once had a really good hunter who came with us for several years in a row. We had a great buck scouted for him, and we had him at about three hundred yards. This buck was huge, and when the hunter saw him he got buck fever bad. I could see the end of his barrel waving, so I told him to hold off, let it go, and we'll come back later.

Harry Leuenberger: You've just got to talk them through it. It takes a lot of communication. I've never had to tell a guy to pass up a shot because of buck fever, because we've often worked tremendously hard to get into position. I figure that some chance is better than no chance at all. But I do my best to get the clients calm through breath control and trigger squeeze.

Nick Frederick: Buck fever to a minor degree is something that we all love to get. I know I do when I get out and hunt for myself, so I guess it's one reason we hunt. It's great to experience that feeling you get only by seeing Mr. Big. There is a form of buck fever, though, that exceeds the fun kind of excitement, and I've seen it many times. I find that the best way to control crippling buck fever in others is to avoid getting the disease myself. After all, the guide isn't carrying the rifle. Personally, I just try to speak clearly and firmly to my clients about what they should do next, because at the moment when the fever has a firm hold on a hunter, processing a lot of information can be next to impossible. Let the client know what to do, but speak in a stern voice. Always communicate with clients so that you know they understand what is going on. A guide must remain in control of the situation in order to be successful. Of course safety is a concern when handling firearms, but when a hunter has buck fever that might be the first thing forgotten. Make the client get a good rest, identify the right buck, and of course keep everything safe.

Mick Chapel: You really can't eliminate buck fever entirely, and the bigger the deer the greater the chance you have of encountering it. About the only answer to it is acquiring hunting experience. Most seasoned hunters have lost the big one at least once. Once, when I was fourteen years old, I was out hunting on horseback with another guy, and we hadn't seen much all day. All of a sudden, about fifty yards in front of me, I saw the head of the biggest mule deer I'd ever seen sticking up above the brush. I dropped my gun, fell off the horse, and then fired five or six times at that buck as it disappeared over the hill. Both of us were shooting, and we missed every time. Even today I grieve over missing that buck of my dreams, a huge typical that was simply awesome. Until you've had that happen and know for certain that you've dropped the ball, until you've fumbled it in the end zone, you can't know how to handle the situation.

The next time you're going to hold onto it with both hands. A seasoned guide can help a client with that problem because he's been there, and if the hunter will listen he can be helped.

Eduardo Gomez Jr.: I have a technique I use that seems to work well. I ask the hunter to put the rifle down, and then I instruct him to take a look at the animal through his binoculars. I tell him to take a deep breath and put the animal again in the riflescope. I also tell him to put the cross hairs on a specific part of the animal and to take his time and not pull the trigger until he is certain of the shot. Specific instruction is necessary in these situations because the hunter has little ability to handle complex situations and calculations if he's beset by buck fever.

David Lopez: I do my best to calm the hunter down so he can shoot accurately. Sometimes that's hard to do if we're looking at a really big deer. If he can't settle down, I try to get him to hold off on the shot until he's calm.

Do you have any wise words on bowhunting? Black powder hunting?

Grant Adkisson: I love bowhunting, and most years it's all I do for my own hunting. My advice on bowhunting is not to buy cheap gear, including arrow rests, broadheads, and sights. Save up and get the very best you can buy. Suffering through poor equipment lasts a lot longer than the thrill of a good price! After that, it takes practice, practice, practice. When I was doing a lot of bowhunting, I was able to shoot a bow almost every day of the year. I've done less black powder hunting, but I'm going to Oregon this year on a black-powder hunt for blacktails.

Jeff Chadd: I don't take a lot of bow hunters. Bow hunters have a different mentality, and this high country is so open it's usually hard to get in range. Black powder is one of my favorite hunts, though, and black-powder season is the very best time of year to hunt these mule deer. Here in Colorado you can't use a scope, but you can still be accurate out to two hundred yards if you practice. Almost everybody shoots either a Thompson Center or a Knight, and they use PowerBelt bullets. They kill some monster bucks, too. I love that time of year because you're up at ten to twelve thousand feet, the bucks are bachelors herded up, and they aren't nearly as spooky. Half the bucks are still in velvet then. To me it's the ultimate hunt.

Robb Wiley: I haven't done a lot of black-powder hunting for mule deer. In my opinion, taking a high-country trophy mule deer buck with a bow is without question the biggest challenge in North American hunting. The wind fluctuates a lot in the high country, and you've got to make a quick stalk before it shifts. That can be a very difficult task.

Keith Atcheson: We have some great bowhunting opportunities for elk and deer on our private ranch in Montana. The best advice I can give to anyone hunting with a bow is to practice, practice, and practice some more, beyond all reason. Don't take quartering angle shots or shoot over forty to fifty yards. Wounding game that escapes is disheartening, and it happens all too frequently in archery hunting. A good bow hunter has superb judgment and practices a great deal. Bowhunting is a lot of fun, but choose your weapon wisely and learn to be good, really good, with your equipment. Black-powder hunting can also be highly effective. With the new technology in black powder rifles, I see very little difference between them and modern centerfire rifles. There are some good black-powder hunts offered in various states that afford a hunter great hunting opportunities that are otherwise not available—and that's probably the smartest thing about being a black-powder hunter.

Doug Gardner: I have a lot to say about bowhunting. We use tree stands, water holes, and the like, but it's sure challenging and fun to hunt mule deer by spot-and-stalk with a bow. The archer shouldn't expect to have his feet firmly planted on level ground at full draw and be able to make the shot without the deer moving or reacting. Bow hunters should practice odd position shooting, up steep hills, down steep hills, off their knees, and off their butts! We do such hunting out in more open country, preferably on a hot, windy day, and we'll get behind those spotting scopes and binoculars and try to find bedded bucks far enough away that they're not threatened by our presence. We often find them up to two miles away. When the bucks are in velvet or just coming out of it, heat and flies are both problems for them, and they pick shady spots that are much more vulnerable than they do when they're in hard antler. If we can get a wind that's blowing into the sun, we're in control and can plan our stalk. You've just got to find a deer you can sneak up on from behind. We have our hunters remove their shoes for the last hundred yards or so to reduce noise, and sometimes there are cacti and rocks to negotiate. We try to find the antler tips sticking up, and many times we're very close. I then back away and let the hunter close in. I use a varmint call to try to get the deer to stand up. If that doesn't work, I move around in front so the deer feels compelled to move but is not spooked. We agree on a hand signal that tells the hunter when to draw, and I try to signal when the deer is just about to stand. The hunter has to remember that he's a predator until he comes to full draw, and then he's got to be an archer. It's really a thrilling way to hunt. We don't have a specific season for black powder in Montana, and hunters with those weapons are in competition with modern firearm hunters. I just tell them that they'll see a lot of deer and they'll have a lot of opportunities, but their choice of weapon is a voluntary limitation that may affect their chances. If we do get some breaks and they get a really good deer they can sure be proud, because they overcame the limitations.

Fred Lamphere: We don't have any black-powder hunters, but we do host a lot of archers. In my personal opinion, they should stay away from expandable broadheads. We've had some bad wounding problems with them, although we have ultimately recovered most of the deer—but sometimes it's two or three days later. My advice is to buy a good conventional broadhead, some for practice and some for the actual hunt. Guys go with the expandable broadheads mainly because they practice with field tips, and the expandables fly a lot like the field points. A good broadhead with a sharp cutting surface is a real killing machine, unlike the expandables. And to return to the question of hunters I won't guide again, I won't guide someone who insists on using expandable broadheads, because I've had such a bad experience with them. I was allowing them four years ago, and two hunters shot their animal the first day out. We collected one of them on the middle of the second day, but it was late on the third day before we finally caught up with the other. They finally got their original animal, but both hunters were packing standard broadheads by then.

Thomas Brunson: Up until a couple of years ago almost all my hunting was bowhunting and black powder hunting, so I have a lot of experience with both. The best tip I can give both kinds of hunters is to put in for those tags because the seasons for those weapons are a lot earlier in the year, both here in Nevada and in most other states. Typically, summer scouting has a lot more effect on those hunts than it does on rifle hunts, which are later in the year. During bow season and black-powder season, the deer are pretty much where they've been spotted through the summer, and that's a huge advantage. The bucks are more out in the open, and their patterns haven't changed from their summer patterns. For the actual hunting, it's again mostly just patience, and you've got to get on the same ridge with them and get right into their business. We watch a buck for a few days before we make a move on him, while we try to figure out the best approach. Sometimes we try to come near the buck in his bed, or else we try to ambush him on the way back to his bed. That applies mainly to bowhunting, and you can't rush it. Black-powder hunting is pretty similar to rifle hunting, except that here in Nevada you can't use a scope on a black-powder rifle. Still, if you practice you can get pretty darned good out to two hundred yards.

Troy Justensen: In Utah there are a lot of terrific opportunities for drawing tags for either category. Here we're able to hunt the pre-rut with a bow, and many muzzleloader hunts are during the rut. These days modern muzzleloaders are on a par with a .308, so it's not too hard to make the shot. In archery, we hunt while the bucks are still in velvet and not nearly so spooky. Most of our hunting is more than 80 percent spot-and-stalk, but with archery we'll sometimes sit over a water hole if the weather is really dry.

Another terrific Colorado buck taken by Jeff Chadd's hunter. (Photo courtesy Jeff Chadd)

Jess Rankin: I do take some muzzleloader hunters for deer. My advice is to buy the best in-line muzzleloader you can. I don't like the antique kind Davy Crockett used at the Alamo. If I remember my Texas history, Davy Crockett didn't fare too well! So get a modern muzzleloader with a scope, if it's legal to use a scope. Some of our muzzleloader hunts in New Mexico require open sights, too. I'd go for something modern that ignites using something other than percussion caps. There are a lot of good ones out there. As far as bowhunting is concerned, it's not a very big part of my business. Again, though, I'd recommend you buy the best equipment you can afford. Also, practice at longer distances than you would for hunting whitetails back East. I get frustrated with hunters who claim that 35 yards is as far as a bow can accurately shoot. Some of my archer friends set their pins for 20, 40, 60, and 80 yards, and they practice at those distances, too. These new, modern bows will shoot that far, with consistency. Our archery mule deer hunts are in January in the heart of the rut, and if you spend the time to stalk a buck, you want to be able to shoot much farther than you generally need to back East, or you might miss your opportunity.

Bowen Dolhan: Do not use mechanical broadheads that can close back up if the buck backs off the arrow a little bit. I'd say not to use anything but flat broadheads, but guys come with what they want to bring and sometimes you just have to live with it. I've simply had too many bad experiences with mechanicals that fold back up. I've seen mechanicals go into the chest cavity, get broken off by the leg, back up a bit, and close completely, so all you've got is essentially a field point in there that is going to do very little cutting. A buck hit with something like that lives far too long and can suffer for three or four hours. If a buck wounded like that gets into the wrong drainage, you're just going to lose him forever. I've seen bucks take three or four hours to die because all they have in the chest cavity is a blunt stick. As for black powder, we don't have a special season for that in Alberta, so we haven't had any black-powder hunters. Unless a person is just a black-powder enthusiast, or there's a special black-powder season that creates a special advantage, there's little reason to use it.

Harry Leuenberger: We do a little bowhunting on elk hunts, but none at all on deer hunts. I have very little to offer in that area.

Nick Frederick: If you can find the time to practice adequately, mule deer can be an excellent animal to bow hunt. They like open country, and thus they often show you their bedding areas. I find it most effective to spot them and then stalk them while they are bedded. After you get within shooting range, wait for the animal to get up and stretch. That's the best time to make your shot. If you try to get in too close or move too fast, you will more than likely spook the buck.

Mick Chapel: Bowhunting mule deer is tough. Most of our bowhunting is stand hunting over a water hole. It's really difficult if you do it any other way. Black powder has some advantages, because you can hunt them in velvet and they aren't nearly as wary or nocturnal. They stand around in the open a lot, and it's just easier to hunt them. The minute they strip that velvet off, though, they become a nocturnal ghost.

Eduardo Gomez Jr.: I don't have any experience with bow hunters, and we do not use black powder in Mexico. I thus have little to offer in those areas.

David Lopez: My opinion on those methods is that they require more patience than other kinds of hunting, and an opportunity may not ever present, no matter how hard we try.

HUNTING MULE DEER WITH THE GUIDES

What constitutes a successful hunt, from your perspective?

Grant Adkisson: A hunt is successful if it's one you enjoy thoroughly. It's successful when you're with quality people in beautiful country, and are prepared the best you can be. Then you can look back on the hunt with fond memories whether you took an animal or not. One of the most successful hunts I've ever been on was a two-week bow hunt for bighorn sheep. I didn't harvest an animal, but that hunt has stuck with me ever since as the epitome of a successful hunt. Picking the right guide and outfitter can contribute a tremendous amount to making your hunt successful.

Jeff Chadd: I don't think a hunter has to kill the biggest buck in the world, but he's got to have a great time and, with luck, kill a decent buck. If he enjoys the hunt I count that as a success, even if for some reason he didn't take a buck.

Robb Wiley: Working as hard as possible and still having fun while you're hunting equals success. If you're having fun it's going to be a successful hunt, regardless of the outcome. That's what we're out there for.

Keith Atcheson: I believe that a successful hunt can be described as a favorable memory and experience. Sharing time in the field with your guide or your family and taking in the whole experience, seeing things you would never see otherwise, sharing hot tea and a toasted sandwich over a midday fire, and reminiscing about past hunts—all those are components of a successful hunt. Success does not necessarily mean you come home with game every time, but that you tried your best and shared some time with people you enjoyed and made a memorable impression that will last. They say that time spent

Would you need a competent guide to tell you which buck to take out of this Alberta field? (Photo courtesy Bowen Dolhan)

hunting and fishing is not counted against your allotted time on earth, so go often!

Doug Gardner: A firm handshake and a smile on the hunter's face is the signal we've had a successful hunt. We really try to get our clients to appreciate the vastness and openness of this eastern Montana ranch country, and the lack of people here. We show them a lot of game. If they're happy with the experience they've had and with the game they've taken, we're certainly happy and feel we've had a successful hunt. If there's dissatisfaction, it's hard to count a hunt as successful, and some people can even turn what should be a successful hunt into an unsuccessful one. They might have taken a really great deer, but if someone else took one a little bit better, they're not happy! But that's too bad. We did our job well; the bad attitude is their fault.

Fred Lamphere: I think if a person leaves here with a good experience of having learned about our area and enjoyed the people, and with a nice trophy, there's no question it's successful. But personality and atmosphere are what bring people back, even more than the quality of your game animals. When it comes down to it, it's a successful hunt if a person enjoys the experience so much that they want to come back, whether they've filled their tag or not.

Thomas Brunson: I think it's been a successful hunt when we have made every attempt to show hunters what they're looking for. Most of my clients want something in the 180⁺ range, and if I've given them an opportunity to fill their tag, that's my measure of success.

Troy Justensen: From my perspective as a guide, I've got to feel that during the hunt I did my best, but also that before the hunt I did my homework, to give the hunter the maximum chance of success. That takes a lot of scouting time. For me to feel the hunt was successful, I've got to control all the factors I can to get a buck for the client, and to feel that we've hunted as hard as we could. Everybody has to feel good about the effort we've put out, whether or not we make a kill.

Jess Rankin: I consider a hunt successful if the hunter goes home happy. Obviously, I'd like to send everybody home with a great trophy, but if you have a good five-day hunt, you see some trophy animals and you're in game, the food is good, the guides are fun to be around, the vehicles don't break down, and the weather is pleasant—I'd say that's a good hunt.

Bowen Dolhan: I count it successful when a hunter leaves happy. I've seen guys go home with huge trophies but who weren't happy for some reason, and you can't count that as a success. I've had guys come up empty-handed. They didn't kill the animal, had a tough hunt, but were really thrilled by the experience. You have to count that as a successful hunt.

Harry Leuenberger: We've got such a variety of game here in the Kootenays that our hunters really get to see a lot. I feel a hunt has been successful if I've given a hunter a reasonable opportunity at a good trophy, whether they got the animal, missed the shot, blew a stalk, or whatever. If I've done my job, that constitutes a successful hunt, and taking a great buck is really just icing on the cake.

Nick Frederick: There are many factors that contribute to a successful hunt. Did you see a good, mature buck that you did not shoot because you already have one that big? Did you enjoy the companionship? Did you see lots of deer? Finally, did you take a buck? After you ask yourself those questions you must fine tune your response. I believe a successful trip is a hunt in which you've seen mature bucks and either tried to harvest them or passed them up looking for something bigger. The trophy hunter should remember that when hunting world-class mule deer you unavoidably pass up bucks that most local hunters wouldn't hesitate to shoot. Really super bucks do not grow on trees, and they are rare even in the best country. They are big because they have made it through enough seasons to have become very wise to danger. A given area can produce only a small number of super bucks in the class we like to take. Remember that when you hunt mule deer for a week or ten days you will learn an awful lot, and that learning experience can certainly be part of a successful outing. The ultimate achievement on a hunt is to take a good buck, of course, and one really feels like more of a winner when there is a buck in the salt. But that doesn't have to happen for the hunt to be a success.

Mick Chapel: You can surely have a successful hunt without killing a deer, and I wish more hunters had that attitude. We beat the country for seven days, we saw some nice deer, maybe it rained three days and the wind blew like crazy, but we hunted hard and we had a good hunt. It's about the hunt, not the kill. I heard it said once that "I kill to have hunted, I don't hunt to kill." It may be a cliché but it's true. You do your best, and it's a success even without a kill. Everybody wants to get the big one, of course, but not everybody will. You know, I've been doing this for a long time, and I'll tell you, things are changing in the world. Hunter quality—and by that I mean the kind of person who can appreciate this truth—is declining dramatically. I don't know what to do about it. Most hunters today are soft. They want to kill the animal, but they don't want to have to hunt very hard. They want to collect a buck as a species, but they aren't interested in the experience of hunting.

Eduardo Gomez Jr.: Success means reaching the goal of hunting a big mule deer and then taking one. However, it's most important that the hunter appreciate good-quality service by all

Sometimes a little foolishness makes for a more memorable hunt. (Photo courtesy Bowen Dolhan)

personnel and staff of the outfitting company. If everyone does a good job, it doesn't necessarily take killing a deer to have a successful hunt.

David Lopez: I count it as successful when we work hard to find the animal and the hunter is tranquil and exhibits a good degree of patience. If the hunter is happy with our effort, it's a successful hunt.

What is the most common mistake made by guided mule deer hunters?

Grant Adkisson: One mistake I find in many kinds of hunting is also common in hunting mule deer: holding out too long. I understand that a hunter is after the best animal he can get, but you must realize that you may see the best animal you're going to see on the first day of the hunt. Many hunters have the idea that they've got to hold out until the very last day in order to take the best animal. If you want to harvest a really good animal, take it when you see it! If you pass up too many you may wind up taking nothing at all, and that's OK for some hunters. For others the harvest is very important, and unless you've got a lot of great mule deer already, you shouldn't pass up an animal that looks really good to you. For a mature hunter who is looking for something special, it's OK to wait, so long as they're being honest about what they expect and about their willingness to go home without a trophy.

Jeff Chadd: All too often hunters don't pay attention to what I'm telling them. They'll walk along the skyline or do something else stupid because they're just not listening to me. The thing about it is that they're paying me for my expertise, and yet they don't listen.

Robb Wiley: Probably the biggest mistake mule deer hunters make is giving up too quickly. The reason is that the bigger, more mature bucks are nocturnal animals that aren't active during daylight hours. You have to be on the top of your game to find them. Another huge mistake is not coming mentally or physically prepared for the challenge. Many hunters don't take the time to practice with their weapon, learn how to get on and off a horse, or learn how to use their gear.

Keith Atcheson: I think that the most common mistake made by guided mule deer hunters is misjudging the size of the deer. Most mule deer hunters think that the deer they're looking at is bigger than it actually is. Having an experienced guide helps on field judging.

Doug Gardner: I think that the most common mistake is not trusting the guide. That's particularly true when it comes to judging deer. Hunters will often either overrule the guide and shoot a deer that's too small, or pass on a deer the guide says is really good.

Fred Lamphere: It's probably shooting too quickly. Even a two- or three-year-old mule deer buck is going to pack a pretty impressive set of antlers. If the hunter has never hunted mule deer before and sees a twenty-four-inch spread on a tinhorn four-point or three-point mule deer, it's pretty easy to pull that trigger. It's inevitable that some will, when they're accustomed to shooting eighty- to ninety-point whitetails.

Thomas Brunson: We frequently have hunters show up in poor condition and with a rifle that's not properly sighted in. That's a bad start to a hunt.

Another great buck taken by Jess Rankin's hunter. (Photo courtesy Jess Rankin)

Troy Justensen: It's very common for hunters to get all hooked up on that 30-inch mark, as though there's something magic about it. I think that's a mistake. I've seen some awfully big deer that are a little narrow, maybe 27 to 28 inches, but because I won't say it's 30 they don't pull the trigger.

Jess Rankin: Shooting poorly is probably the most frequent mistake hunters make, often by shooting under the animal at long distances. I've had guys who were afraid to shoot at a deer at three hundred yards, too. There's that phrase again: "I'm not comfortable shooting at something three hundred yards away." Well, just aim right at them and shoot! It's no different than shooting at them at one hundred yards, except that the target is only a third as big.

Bowen Dolhan: In my experience, it's been passing on real trophy bucks because it's early in the hunt. Sometimes I spend thirty to forty days looking to find a really good buck, and because they see the animal on the first day they pass it up! They're thinking that if they see this kind of animal on the first day, what will they see if they hold out? It's a big mistake to pass just because it's the first or second day. Whatever day of the hunt it is, if the guide tells you that's the one, then that's the one! Trust him and shoot!

Harry Leuenberger: In the past, the most common thing was not listening to the guide's estimate of the distance. Now we've got rangefinders, so that isn't as important. Today it's probably being antsy and moving around too much while we're up there glassing. You've got to stay still or any deer will see you before you see them.

Nick Frederick: The most common mistake made by mule deer hunters is thinking that everybody in camp will kill a 200+ buck. While our mule deer camps have been highly successful, with that success comes some level of frustration as well. We have photo albums full of pictures of big bucks that we have taken over the years. Hunters must remember that when they go on a guided hunt they are still on a hunt, and that implies a level of uncertainty. It is always nice when someone kills a big buck early in the week, because everybody then knows that they have not been tricked into coming to our camp. They know they are in the right place and can hope that a big one shows for them, too.

Mick Chapel: Overestimating the size of a buck is very common, especially if it jumps up and is running away from you. By the same token, though, if you don't shoot he's not going to give you a chance to look him over. It can be a dilemma.

Eduardo Gomez Jr.: It's very common for the hunter not to judge the animal well. On the guide's side, sometimes they push the hunter to shoot too quickly.

David Lopez: That's when they waste time trying to track the animal on their own. I am trained and experienced at tracking desert mule deer, so why should the hunter concern himself with doing my job?

What can a guided hunter do that would most improve the chances of taking game (patience, physical fitness, mental preparation, equipment, practice with choice of weapon, other)?

Grant Adkisson: All the points you list are important. I would encourage hunters to realize they're going on a guided hunt and that time is limited. It's not like being back home, where they can go out another day and try another stand. A guided hunt is of much shorter duration, and they need to keep that in mind. They should be mentally prepared to enjoy every aspect of the hunt whether they take an animal or not. They should have in mind that they're going to enjoy being outdoors and take pleasure in the scenery and fellowship with other hunters, and try to put the kill far down on the list. If they do that, and they buy the best equipment they can afford and practice with it so they're ready for their opportunity, they'll have a great hunt no matter what. I find that this type of hunter always has the greatest chance of success. Another thing I'd strongly recommend is that hunters not change anything at the last minute. For example, I had a hunter miss a tremendous opportunity at an outstanding buck just seventy yards away while he tried to figure out how to use a bipod he'd attached to his rifle only the day before. Stick with what you've been using in practice so you're thoroughly familiar with it, and you won't have something like that happen to you.

Jeff Chadd: You hit it on the head with all of the things you listed. You've got to be mentally prepared to sit on a buck for three or four days. Three years ago we hunted a huge buck during black-powder season, and we finally got on him the very last hour of the last day. That's the value of patience. That buck scored 202!

Robb Wiley: By far the biggest factor is being mentally prepared. I've been privileged to hunt all the Western states, as well as Mexico, for mule deer. It's always a challenging hunt for trophy animals. That's especially so because there aren't that many real trophies. If you aren't prepared for the mental challenges of such a hunt, you might just as well give it up.

Keith Atcheson: Hunters can improve their chances of taking game by mentally and physically practicing all aspects of the hunt. Some of the most physically fit hunters I have ever hunted with, some of them incredible physical specimens, melted like cotton candy when they got out in the field. That occurred simply because they were not mentally prepared for a difficult hunt. Mental preparation comes with physical conditioning plus experience on previous adventures. Once in a while we get hunters who have absolutely no experience yet want to jump into some of the most difficult hunts in the world, such as polar bear, or Marco Polo argali. It's always a pretty high risk, and most of the time it's a disaster. Work your way up the ladder and get to know yourself well.

Doug Gardner: If I had to choose one of these, I'd say mental preparation. If a guy really wants a good trophy he has to come with the mindset that he's got to take advantage of his opportunity whenever it comes. That can be early, when he's not expecting it, or late in the hunt, when the tendency is to be discouraged but he's still got to be at the top of his game.

Fred Lamphere: I tell my hunters to get in shape by walking and stretching. Walk up some hills and stretch those leg muscles. That's about as physical as we need to be, because we're not rock climbers and we're not sheep hunters. Mental preparation is important, however: doing things like studying mule deer books, looking at different rack configurations, and visiting a taxidermy shop and holding some antlers in your hands. Then practice shooting quickly at different ranges. Find the method that is going to be comfortable for you. If you just can't shoot consistently offhand at 100 or 150 yards, see if you can do it at 75 yards. Don't just bench shoot; do it like you're really hunting. Be comfortable with your rifle, and don't go out and buy something new just for this hunt. You might not have enough time to develop the experience and confidence in it that you need.

Thomas Brunson: That's a pretty good list, and I agree with everything in the question as being important. Also, learning to listen to the guide is a high priority in my book, because there's a reason for everything he does. Hunters need to trust whatever he says.

Troy Justensen: I'm really big on hunters practicing with their choice of weapon. When it comes time to make the shot, you've got to come through, because a chance at a truly trophy mule deer might not come around again.

Jess Rankin: Practicing would be number one. Hunters need to learn to shoot in a variety of situations, too, at the least using a bipod from a prone position.

Ask the Mule Deer Guides

Bowen Dolhan: All of the above, for sure, as well as just being ready whenever an opportunity presents. A lot of guys go into the day with their game in the off position. Being ready should be a part of being out in the field. That falls somewhat under the heading of mental preparation, but it really covers everything else, too.

Harry Leuenberger: Being in the right spot is best, and a little luck sure doesn't hurt. That aside, patience and physical fitness are number one and number two, especially in our hunting area. Practice with the weapon comes in a very close third. I sure hate it when a hunter shows up with no idea of where his gun is shooting. Mental preparation is difficult, because there's no way to be certain what you're facing on the hunt until you're actually there. Equipment is covered well in our operation because we give hunters a comprehensive list of what they need.

Nick Frederick: The hunter should target practice at home as much as possible. There is nothing more frustrating than working hard all week to find a big buck and then missing or placing a shot poorly. I know that we all miss and it's part of the game, but there is sometimes no excuse for some of the poor shooting I've seen. There's no substitute for plenty of practice. Having faith in your guide and trusting him is also very important. If you do and things still go wrong, then you have chosen the wrong outfitter and can mark it down as a lesson learned. However, many times I have heard hunters blame a guide for not doing this or not doing that. Just remember there are always two sides to any story.

Mick Chapel: Everything you've listed is very important. I'd add to that to be very careful when you're hiring a guide. Do your homework. There are so many guides out there that are nothing more than shysters. I hate to say that, but it's true. Be very careful of a guaranteed kill, because there's no such thing on a free-chase hunt.

Eduardo Gomez Jr.: I'd rate the first and last on your list as tops. Patience is absolutely necessary in order to be successful and come to the point of taking a good trophy. Practice with the weapon then comes into play, because if you miss when your opportunity comes, it's most often all over.

David Lopez: In Sonora the most important factors are the right area and a competent guide. Everything else we can work around, but if there isn't a big deer in the area, we're wasting our time.

Besides the weapon, what kind of equipment should every hunter carry? And besides the weapon, what is the most important single piece of equipment?

Grant Adkisson: Great optics is the answer to that question, particularly your riflescope. Don't go cheap on it, or on your spotting scope, your binoculars, or whatever. I also think that shooting sticks are important, so long as you've practiced with them. A rangefinder is also a priority, though your guide may have one. I recommend that hunters carry them, too.

Jeff Chadd: The answer to both questions is binoculars of the best quality a person can afford. You must have good glass to look through, because some days we glass for twelve to fourteen hours. You don't want to be dealing with junk.

Robb Wiley: The best optics you can afford is the answer to both questions.

Keith Atcheson: The single most important piece of equipment besides your trustworthy firearm is a good pair of binoculars, and close behind that is a quality spotting scope. Many clients come out hunting with fine rifles and scopes, but they've got a pair of $39.99 binoculars. That amazes me. Spend as much as you possibly can on good optics. It will make you a better hunter because you will use your optics more, you will see more, and you will inevitably take more game.

Doug Gardner: Layered clothing is a must, because the weather can sure be changeable here. Good footwear is also imperative. Still, the most important equipment is optics, both in binoculars and riflescope. If hunters don't have these, they won't be able to see what the guide is trying to show them. I've had hunters show up with $3,000 rifles topped with a bargain

Following the guide's instructions can lead to a great buck like this South Dakota giant. (Photo courtesy Fred Lamphere)

store scope! We can help a lot with our binoculars, but we can't help if the riflescope is of poor quality.

Fred Lamphere: Good optics is number one in my book. I've graduated through the ranks of affordability, being just a ranch kid out here in South Dakota and buying whatever I could manage. The first time I spent $100 on a pair of binoculars, I thought I was buying a Cadillac. Now I use Leica optics, both their binoculars and their spotting scope. I'll give Leupold a plug for their riflescopes, because I think they're premium in that category. I say spend the money and get good optics, because it's an investment for your whole life.

Thomas Brunson: Good optics is the most important single piece of equipment, especially when combined with the ability to use them competently. I don't go anywhere in our country without my knives, rain gear, flashlight, first-aid kit, and the like, because out here you never know what's going to happen. Water is a real problem on our backpack hunts, because we're hunting along ridgelines at ten thousand to eleven thousand feet, and the water is down in the bottom of the basin a few thousand feet lower. It's pretty tough sometimes to pack enough water.

Troy Justensen: I'd say good binoculars and a rangefinder. You can rely on the guide for finding the deer, but it's nice to participate yourself and maybe find the buck yourself. However, when the final stalk comes, the guide might not be in position to tell you the exact distance with his own rangefinder. That's particularly true of archery hunters, but it's also important to know the distance of a long rifle shot. I'd put pretty much the same stock in good optics and a good rangefinder.

Jess Rankin: Good binoculars are pretty important, though unfortunately some of my hunters rely completely on the guide for glassing. When hunting the West it's really important to be able to glass. Another item I'd rate highly is good footwear that won't cause blisters if you have to do some walking.

Bowen Dolhan: For bow hunters it's a rangefinder, and don't be scared to use it. Even if you miss the opportunity because you were taking the range, it's still a lot better than not using it. The tendency is to say, "Oh, he's there, I've got no time to use it." Well, if he gets away because you were checking the range, that's good compared with shooting over the top of him or, even worse, having a wounded deer on your hands. For rifle hunters, it's a toss-up between a spotting scope, good binoculars, and shooting sticks. You've got to have a rest. A spotting scope will save you a lot of leg work, and sometimes you just don't have a good enough view through binoculars.

Harry Leuenberger: We live behind our binoculars, so that's the answer to both your questions.

Nick Frederick: It is a good idea to carry binoculars, since you will be glassing and looking for a buck. After the buck has been spotted and you have decided you are going to try to take it, the hunter can generally put the binoculars away. On more than one occasion I have physically taken binoculars away from my client, because on the stalk it is the guide's job to be looking for the deer. Many times hunters are fumbling with their binoculars while the deer is in range for a shot. I have turned around to see if my hunter is getting ready to take a shot to find they are trying to focus their binoculars. After you get on the deer, the only optics the hunter needs is the riflescope. A bipod is good for longer shots, and most of the time while mule deer hunting you

A mighty mule deer taken in velvet by a beautiful lady guided by Grant Adkisson.
(Photo courtesy Grant Adkisson)

have time to open up the device and steady yourself for a secure shot. Rangefinders are good, too, but in my opinion they should usually be handled by the guide.

Mick Chapel: Your binoculars are extremely important, so have good ones.

Eduardo Gomez Jr.: Like most of the guides you've interviewed, I'd rate good optics right at the top. You've got to be able to find the deer and evaluate it before you can shoot it.

David Lopez: Good boots are extremely important, because you already know we're going to be doing a lot of walking. Next come good binoculars, and after that effective camouflage clothing.

Are there any common items of equipment that you feel are unnecessary, redundant, or just plain worthless for hunting mule deer?

Grant Adkisson: One thing that's worthless is one of those large, padded, thickly insulated jump suits. They may work for some kinds of hunting, where you're sitting in a blind or on a stand or riding a snowmobile. But we are constantly on the move, and our hunters must have extreme flexibility in their clothing. Under one of those jump suits a guy may be wearing only long underwear, and he's stuck with that heavy clothing no matter how much walking and climbing we have to do. We advise our hunters to dress in many layers so they can put on and take off clothing as necessary.

Jeff Chadd: Hunter orange! I hate that stuff! I come down here after guiding in Alaska, where nobody wears it, and all of a sudden I've got to put on this ridiculous orange rig. Up in the high country you can see forever, and a hunter stands out like the Statue of Liberty. Hunter orange is just a legal requirement that does nobody any good whatsoever where I hunt! We wear it because it's required, but out here it's very nearly worthless.

Robb Wiley: A GPS is the most worthless piece of equipment imaginable in the mountains. I've got an internal guidance system that helps me to kill big mule deer by allowing me to navigate around the mountains and remember the exact spots I need

Guides can give excellent advice and encouragement when stalking a giant like this one. (Photo courtesy Jess Rankin)

to find again. A GPS just gets me lost! I believe a GPS in the mountains gets people into trouble far more than it helps them, because it calls for you to go in straight lines. If you try to run a straight course in the mountains, you're going to wind up on a cliff or up a canyon where you can't get out.

Keith Atcheson: Nothing really outstanding comes to mind that's totally worthless.

Doug Gardner: I guess there's a lot of stuff that's not much use here, but it boils down to the personal choice of the hunter. I try not to criticize nonessential toys that hunters bring with them, unless they're likely to interfere with our chances of success.

Fred Lamphere: There are so many knickknacks today for mule deer hunters. It's not as bad as turkey hunting, but there are still a lot. There are always new things for sale. I guess what I'd recommend, especially on a guided hunt, is a minimum of gadgets. Your guide is going to have a rangefinder, or else he'll be darn good at estimating the distance. I can't say you shouldn't have a rangefinder, but sometimes spending time to check the range and lock in the exact distance can be a golden minute lost. I'd just say keep gadgets to a minimum, have good binoculars, have good footwear, and have a good rifle.

Thomas Brunson: Shooting sticks can come in handy, but for our kind of hunting they're not very useful most of the time. Other than that, I can't think of anything major.

Troy Justensen: I've given this question some thought, and nothing truly worthless comes to mind. We live in a world of gadgets, so let the hunter enjoy them.

Jess Rankin: Nothing that's totally worthless comes to mind.

Bowen Dolhan: I can't recall anything people are bringing that stands out as unnecessary. There's a gadget or two every year that people don't need, but no single thing is prevalent.

Harry Leuenberger: I've thought a lot about that question, and I guess you don't need an elk bugle when hunting mule deer! No, really, I can't come up with any gadgets that are totally worthless if a guy wants to bring them. A GPS is pretty much useless, but if a hunter wants to have one just for fun, that's OK.

Nick Frederick: Not that I can think of right off hand.

Mick Chapel: Just don't carry a lot of junk. Beyond your weapon and your binoculars, you need a really good camera. The best way to tell if a person is a serious trophy hunter is by looking at their camera. If a hunter shows up with no camera or a throwaway job, you can bet he's not a serious trophy hunter, and more likely a novice. I like to look at the camera setup, because it tells me volumes about the hunter's expectations.

Eduardo Gomez Jr.: Face paint, camouflage gloves, and scents to cover human odor are all pretty worthless, in my opinion. I'd rate cover scents as the most worthless of these.

David Lopez: I hate to see a hunter show up with a heavy backpack and binoculars half as big as a car. It's a struggle to carry all that. Hunters need to travel light so we have a chance of finding the real monster mule deer.

Same old story: Good optics are needed to find and take the best animals.

How do you evaluate a location for its potential to produce big mule deer bucks?

Grant Adkisson: I use the record books a lot. It doesn't always help, but if I've already taken a lot of good bucks and I want to find a really special one, I'd look at the record book to see where the big ones live. It's a really good use for the record books, and it's one good reason why I belong to the organizations that publish them. Those books are a tremendous resource for the hunting community that many people don't recognize. I also pay attention to stories about big bucks that come out in the magazines. If you look and find out where they're consistently harvesting big bucks, it probably merits booking a hunt there. A secondary technique I use is phone calls to successful hunters, and it's surprising how often you can run them down and get them on the phone. I also wouldn't hesitate to call an outfitter or the state game department for information.

Jeff Chadd: I do a tremendous amount of scouting. I go to places that are overlooked where there's no pressure. I went into one drainage last year where there were eight bucks, and two of them were giants. One of the pair was a real cranker. I basically stay off the beaten path and try to find those pockets where nobody else thinks to go.

Robb Wiley: The best indicator of a big buck is when one is standing in the area! That's definitely the best way. We do a lot of preseason scouting and we look for a lot of things—tracks, sign, cover, food, and so on. There are definitely places big muley bucks hole up, but they're all different for different bucks. The things they have in common are convenient food sources, light human activity, and a secure place to bed.

Keith Atcheson: It's a combination of good genetics, reflected in what the area has produced in the past, plus limited hunting pressure, either because it's private land or it's so remote there's no easy access.

Doug Gardner: Mule deer have a lot of requirements, but chief among them is a place where they can grow old. If there's a lot of hunting pressure, it takes a special deer to live to be five years old. After that, he becomes much more capable of surviving to be a really old animal. Genetics are important, but they don't do any good if the deer doesn't get old enough to take advantage of its genes. Look for a place where a deer will be likely to grow old without getting shot.

Fred Lamphere: I like to go out first thing in the spring and hunt shed antlers. I also like to visit with the locals, because if big bucks are coming from an area it's likely to produce more. But it's hard to go to a ranch and judge whether big deer are there just by the way the place looks. I've gone to ranches and wondered why any deer would live there, and then my jaw hits the sagebrush when I get out and start looking around. I often can't figure out what drew them in there, but after a while you start to put it all together. The most important aspect is the history of a place, what it's produced before, because that tells a lot about its potential. Lack of pressure plus quality habitat equals good bucks, assuming the genetics are there. If there's too much hunting pressure, that leads to nomadic activity and the deer are gone.

Thomas Brunson: I look for a place that has isolation, good food and cover, and water. Once I find a spot like that, I go back and check it frequently in the summer to see if it holds a good buck. In the summer big bucks are more out in the open, and these muley bucks are pretty territorial. They will still be there until the rut begins. Even when the rifle hunts start bucks still don't leave their home area; they just get a little tighter back into the brush.

Troy Justensen: Here in Utah, the area's history is the most important thing. If it has produced big muleys in the past, it probably still has good potential. You can get that information from the game department, but it's probably more easily available from the Boone and Crockett Club's record book, which lists the counties in which bucks were taken.

Jess Rankin: There are several factors to consider. One is deer density, and another is the buck to doe ratio. Then there's the number of older age bucks in the area and the roughness of the terrain. A final critical matter is how hard it is to get a tag there.

Bowen Dolhan: To produce good numbers of trophy bucks that can actually be taken, an area must have an adequate overall population of mule deer, good food sources, high genetic potential, low hunting pressure, and good enough size. For lots of mule deer bucks to reach full potential by growing old, they need a massive amount of land to roam: not just a two-by-four-mile place, but fifty to a hundred square miles. In such an area there are some rough hiding places, some wicked drainages where they can grow old because they can't be easily found.

Harry Leuenberger: I've been hunting in there for thirty-five years, so we know the country and the deer so well that we can predict where they live, where they'll migrate, and where they'll winter. We pretty much know where they hang out all the time, so we don't do a lot of pondering when it comes to evaluating a particular site. In fact, in the high basins it's a lot like hunting sheep. We've been here for so long that the question has little meaning for our operation.

Nick Frederick: Finding an area that produces big bucks can come only from experience. Of course, that doesn't mean you couldn't go out deer hunting the first time and shoot a 190 buck, but that would be more luck than anything. When you can take one client every year to a certain section of land and know you have a good chance of seeing a big buck, that comes only from experience. We all know that certain provinces and states are historically good for trophy mule deer, but that is just the starting point. Alberta is a big place, and if I suggested you go there and you didn't know exactly where to look, you could travel for quite some time before you found what you were looking for. In our area I have some ranches that produce one or two super bucks a year (spotted but not always killed). These ranches are sometimes only two thousand acres or less, and you a need great deal of space to produce big mule deer bucks. But even though that's true, there are very small areas that seem to have just the right combination of factors to produce one or two big bucks year after year. There are other places, only a few miles down the road, that almost never produce any big bucks. Some of the biggest bucks

Ask the Mule Deer Guides

I have guided for have come from within a four-mile radius that has a lot of open space around it.

Mick Chapel: That's hard to say. What I look for more than anything is country that's huntable. You get down in Mexico and you've got this big six-mile valley where the visibility is a few yards through the brush, and there's not an elevation, not a knob, not a tree, nothing, in the whole place. There's just no way you can hunt it. I go somewhere else. I don't care if there's a 290-inch buck in such a place; you're not going to get him. That's some of that country I mentioned earlier, where it's just not possible to overhunt the area because you can't hunt it at all.

Eduardo Gomez Jr.: We use a number of techniques to determine where to find big bucks. We thoroughly scout the area, and we look at the results of prior hunts as to quantity and size of bucks. In Sonora, if it's as dry as it usually is, we also check tracks and activity around available water holes.

David Lopez: If I find the tracks of a big mule deer, that's the best indicator. If I see a big mule deer, that's the only thing that's better. All of Sonora has conditions that produce good mule deer, but some areas are hunted too hard and other areas don't offer enough cover. In some places, there's too much cover.

Chapter 6

HUNTING IN THE ROCKY MOUNTAIN WEST FOR MULE DEER

Describe your home guiding area for mule deer.

Grant Adkisson: I live right where I was raised, and we're at about five thousand feet elevation in the piñon-juniper region of Colorado. There are a lot of draws or arroyos. There is a lot of rimrock country, and those big bucks will lie underneath that overhang; you can't see them from above, but they can see everything below them. At times I'm in aspen/pine country, and occasionally I'm out on the eastern plains of Colorado in wheat country. The hunting is entirely different there. I've also guided timberline hunts, and those, too, are pretty different from my home area.

Jeff Chadd: Our hunting area is basically scrub oak and what I call pucker brush; it's the high country of central Colorado. In the early season, we're hunting from eight thousand up to twelve thousand feet, and last year I killed a buck at thirteen thousand feet. It's steep, mountainous terrain, and it's rough, rocky, and rugged. Hunting with me you'd think you were sheep hunting, because it reminds me a lot of the places where we do hunt sheep. This is primarily muzzleloader hunting. Later, we move down to around eight or nine thousand feet and lower sagebrush country for the rifle season.

Robb Wiley: It's the western Wyoming high country. We have ten-thousand-foot peaks, big, high valleys cutting between the mountains, and very open optics-friendly country. It's very cliffy, with steep drop-offs, vertical walls of rock, high mountain basins, dark timber in the lower areas, patches of quakies cutting the mountainsides, sagebrush foothills, and so on. It's a real slice of the Rocky Mountains from the foothills to the peaks.

Take 'em early and take 'em in velvet in Colorado. (Photo courtesy Grant Adkisson)

What are some distinctions that set it apart?

Grant Adkisson: One is that often you can get up high and watch for animals, and then wait for them to bed before you make your stalk. In some areas the terrain isn't conducive to that, but here it is. It's possible because you can see so much territory from a good vantage point.

Jeff Chadd: It's high, tough hunting. It's also hard to draw in some of the best areas, so you sometimes need to accumulate more points before you get a tag. We've got a really great mule deer population right now, and we're running close to fifty bucks per hundred does. The thing that could ruin it is the Division of Wildlife, because in my opinion they're going to issue too many tags. It's a shame, because right now Colorado is the poster child for bringing back the mule deer. It just irritates me to death that they want to issue more tags, with the success of the current program so obvious. Why they want to screw it up, I'll never understand. I was just looking at the Boone and Crockett bucks taken in the last five years, and Colorado doubles the next closest state. I sure hope that cooler heads prevail and they keep the program as is.

Robb Wiley: It has great mule deer genetics, and it's as rugged as mule deer country comes.

Why should a hunter hire a guide, as opposed to being self-guided?

Grant Adkisson: If you want to be successful, it's worth the expense. Self-guided hunts are fine, but the facts speak for themselves: The success rate is far higher with a guide.

Jeff Chadd: Because I know the area. I live here! Sure, a guy who draws a mule deer tag in this area is going to kill a buck of some kind, because if he doesn't he shouldn't be hunting. We've

A great drop-tine buck taken with Jeff Chadd. (Photo courtesy Jeff Chadd)

The ladies keep dropping fine bucks. (Photo courtesy Jeff Chadd)

got the deer here. But to kill the trophy deer he wants and that he's spent his points to draw, he really needs me. I scout all the time, and I can find him that deer of his dreams. I think a guy with one of those precious tags in hand is crazy to try to save a few bucks by not hiring a guide. I'll be scouting all summer, and I guarantee you I'll know where there are some dandy bucks.

Robb Wiley: I'd say that by hiring a guide you're going to up your chances considerably. I must add that this isn't true of some outfitters, who are there for the wrong reasons, even though they wear the hat. Most really good outfitters, though, are definitely going to improve your odds. They do that in great part simply by instilling confidence in the hunter and supporting that all-important positive attitude.

What is your success rate on trophy animals?

Grant Adkisson: To me, any animal is a trophy to be appreciated as a unique creation of God, even a doe. If you're basing the term "trophy" on making the record book, and that's what you're serious about, I'd say it depends on the kind and price of hunt you book. Our private-land hunts are expensive, but they are conducted on a big spread that's managed for trophy deer and elk and the success rate approaches 100 percent. We took a guy on his first mule deer hunt to that ranch last season, and he landed a buck that gross scored 223. We could take more hunters, but that ranch is the very best. We keep it that way by severely limiting the take and keeping our success rate high. The place is high country with gorgeous aspens and pines, and the hunting is outstanding. On our public land hunts and some ranch hunts, I guarantee good food and accommodations, and we have a very high success rate on those hunts, too. I never promise a certain size or class of animal, but I'll send a person a photo of all the animals we took last year, from the smallest to the largest, if they want it, and they can decide if we're offering what they're looking for. We do have a high success rate for great trophy animals, but as I said before, I prefer to undersell and overproduce.

Another real Colorado monster taken on a hunt with Jeff Chadd. (Photo courtesy Jeff Chadd)

A monster taken in the snow with Robb Wiley. (Photo courtesy Robb Wiley)

Hunting in the Rocky Mountain West for Mule Deer

Jeff Chadd: I have not sent a hunter home from Colorado without a deer. We're 100 percent. I've had a couple of people in Montana who didn't get a deer, but even there it's rare. I would say, though, that the trophy is in the eye of the beholder, and we had one handicapped guy who shot a 175 buck and was tickled to death with it. Most of our deer are larger than that.

Robb Wiley: We run about 40 to 50 percent true trophy mule deer, and by "trophy" I mean one of our giants. If you go to many parts of Montana and kill a 170-inch mule deer, you've killed a big one. Here, we're just getting started at 170 inches. We could be at 100 percent if we were just killing four-point bucks, but we're seeking a certain age class of deer. It's not all a question of how many points a buck has, nor even how it will score, because some bucks with a fork-horn frame will have a dozen extra atypical points and they're fantastic trophies. We chased one we called "Captain Hook" because he had a two-point main frame, but he was an 11x7 because he had all those extra points. He was a real whopper that wouldn't score very well.

Describe your usual hunting method and any common variations.

Grant Adkisson: All of our hunting is spot-and-stalk, if the hunter is able. In open areas, whether high country, piñon-juniper country, or just open agricultural country, we try to get to a high point and glass a lot. The biggest success I've had with mule deer hunting is to spot the animal first and then plan an approach to within range after it beds. You can't just walk through an area hoping to see something, because you'll just spook the deer. We sometimes have to wait until the next day, and we may have to drive to another starting place to get within walking distance, but that's how we locate an animal we want to take.

Jeff Chadd: We get out in the morning and get up to our glassing spot before daylight. In some areas we have four-wheel-drive trails that will get us pretty close, but in others it's a long climb. In any event we're there before daylight, and at the crack of dawn we're glassing our eyes out. If we find a good buck we put

They don't come much heavier than this Rocky Mountain monarch. (Photo courtesy Robb Wiley)

a stalk on him and try to get close enough for a shot. If he's in a bad place, we just have to wait until he cooperates. Our average shot with a modern rifle is 200 yards. With a muzzleloader I try to get within 120 yards, and sometimes with a big bachelor herd of two dozen bucks, it can be hard to pick out which one is the big guy. Then, too, we've got almost fifty eyes watching for us.

Robb Wiley: When a hunter shows up we're hunting specific animals, because we've usually located the one we want to hunt by our preseason scouting. We take the hunter to a specific vantage point to look for that animal. We keep changing our vantage point until we find the deer we want.

Do you use any special techniques, such as rattling, grunting, or doe-in-heat lure?

Grant Adkisson: Some people have tried rattling and say it works, but I'm not a big fan of it and don't use it. We do some rattling for elk, and I've used it successfully for whitetails in other places. None of the other things are good for mule deer.

Jeff Chadd: The thing I like to do that's special is to get behind and above the deer. It's just like hunting sheep, as I've said before. Last year we found a really big buck during muzzleloader season, and he and his five buddies lay at the end of a big plateau for two days. It was a spot that was just impossible to approach, at 12,500 feet of elevation. I told the hunter that if they ever bailed off to feed below that rim, we were going to get him. Well, on the last day they did exactly that, so we took off and got to the spot where they had been. It wasn't even a long shot down the slope to the deer, and we got him! He had been king of the mountain, but now he's king of somebody's trophy room!

Robb Wiley: No, it's all optics.

How do you hunt differently when with a client/hunter, as opposed to when hunting alone (for yourself)?

Grant Adkisson: Most of the time I cover a lot less ground with a client. Of course, I encourage clients ahead of time to be in the best possible shape so we can get around well, but it's not always possible. I also push myself a lot harder on my own hunts because, if I've seen a great animal, I'm not concerned about getting back by mealtime or even sleeping in camp. I always take the client's comfort and security into consideration more than I do my own.

Jeff Chadd: I guess I'm a lot more careful, because I go into some pretty rough places by myself that I just wouldn't take a client into. I hunt pretty hard, too, more so than with a client.

For a combination of heavy and wide, they don't come much better than this giant muley. (Photo courtesy Robb Wiley)

Robb Wiley: I really don't do anything differently, except that I can often get around better without a client. When I'm alone I leave the horse tied up somewhere and hunt on foot, but when I have a client I often have to take the horses.

What time of the season offers the best hunting in your area (and the highest possibility of success on trophy animals)?

Grant Adkisson: Big mule deer are much more visible when they're in velvet, even though most places you can't hunt them at that time. It's a guess on my part, but it's probably uncomfortable for them to go through heavy brush when those antlers are covered with sensitive velvet, so they stay out in the open more. With Colorado's Ranching for Wildlife Program, we do have the opportunity to hunt those bucks in velvet with a rifle in September, and it's a great time to hunt. The other time big bucks are visible is, of course, during the rut, when they have lost all caution. We have some great hunts in November.

Jeff Chadd: If I had a choice, I'd hunt the muzzleloader season. They just brought back the rut hunt last year and it's good, but to me the experience of being up high with good weather in September far outshines any other time.

Robb Wiley: It's always good, anytime, from start to finish. There's no rhyme or reason to it, usually, and it's often like determining who's going to win the lottery. The key is to come and give it 100 percent effort while you're here, because there really is no secret as far as the timing of the hunt.

How much does weather influence hunting success in your area?

Grant Adkisson: It's usually not a big factor unless there's fog. We can handle hot weather, cold weather, snow, or whatever, but fog will shut us down. If you can't glass them, you just can't hunt them.

Jeff Chadd: It depends entirely on the snow. If we get snow early and we're trying to hunt the high country, it can make the hunting very tough. With snow the deer simply disperse and are impossible to find.

Robb Wiley: It has some influence, but two of the biggest bucks we've ever killed were taken by a father and son, one scoring 197 inches and the other 205, on a full moon phase with midday temperatures of 80 degrees and an extreme drought. It was the most difficult hunting picture you can imagine, but we killed two giants. So you can't say that the weather is always a big factor.

How much do weather and time of season influence where and how you hunt?

Grant Adkisson: Unless there's a heavy snowstorm, such as on a hunt in late November, it doesn't change our location or technique very much. You can't do much hunting in a blizzard, but other than that we just stay out and hunt by spot-and-stalk.

Jeff Chadd: They definitely have a big effect. If we get snow, I get pushed out and I've just got to regroup. I may have to go to some lower stuff or some private ranches I hunt. Sometimes, though, the really big bucks will stay right up top in waist-deep snow, just like a big elk. I saw a big buck three years ago at around twelve thousand feet in snow you wouldn't believe, and it was the third season.

Robb Wiley: They do influence us a little, because if there's fog and bad weather we've got to change tactics. We simply can't use long-distance glassing to find the deer. However, clearing weather can be some of the most productive hunting.

What can a self-guided hunter do to maximize his chances of taking a good mule deer buck?

Grant Adkisson: He should do the most research he possibly can. He needs to contact successful hunters if at all possible and see what they did. Also, call the state game and fish people and get their thoughts. The Internet has also become a great resource for people looking for a good self-guided hunt.

Jeff Chadd: I'd say he needs to really get to know the area. Come scout the area, look at maps, and maybe even talk to a biologist. Get knowledgeable about the area so you can have a good chance. I know that's hard advice to take if a hunter is from New York and he's going to hunt in Colorado, but unless you study and know the area you'd better hire a guide. The draw takes place the first of June, so a person who draws has the whole summer, and maybe a good bit of the fall, to get out and do some scouting. The part about high country hunting that's tough is that bucks you find there in the summer won't be in the same place after the snows come or after they rub off the velvet. They become a totally different animal in a totally different location.

Robb Wiley: In our country, a person who is going to have a decent shot at being successful on his own needs to dedicate a month of time to coming out early and doing the necessary preseason scouting. He needs to be really familiar with the country, or he'd be better off hiring an outfitter.

Chapter 7

HUNTING ON THE HIGH PLAINS
FOR MULE DEER

Describe your home guiding area for mule deer.

Keith Atcheson: Our home guiding area for mule deer is in central Montana, north of Lewistown. The area is game rich with hundreds of mule deer, pronghorn antelope, a very good herd of elk, and some decent white-tailed deer. It's rolling land with some steep high country thrown in.

Doug Gardner: The ranches we hunt, both our own ranch and those we lease, have good deer as well as good cattle. Eastern Montana is completely different from the rest of the world, because not many people have a backyard this big to play in. Some of the ranches we lease are immense, and that's what it takes to have a lot of deer hunting. People who hunt with me call me a good manager, while the people who don't want to pay the freight drive down the road and see the posted signs and don't think much of me. But there's no other way to have the quality of deer hunting we offer except by limiting access.

Fred Lamphere: We've got mostly open sagebrush and brushy drainages that flow into small prairie rivers. It's rolling sagebrush hills mixed with river breaks and badlands.

What are some distinctions that set it apart?

Keith Atcheson: The quality of our mule deer stays high because all permits are obtained by the draw. Our mule deer licenses in Montana are a guaranteed license when booking with an outfitter, so clients don't have to worry about drawing a tag. Much of the hunting is done by four-wheel-drive and on foot. We can handle virtually anyone, from the guy hunting in a wheelchair to someone who is physically fit and wants to go to the top.

Another great Montana muley taken with Keith Atcheson. (Photo courtesy Keith Atcheson)

Doug Gardner: In short, it's the genetics of our deer and the fact that it's predominantly private land where we can control the harvest.

Fred Lamphere: I think it's the diversity of the terrain. On one ten-thousand-acre ranch, you can go from pancake flat river bottom to steep badlands in less than a mile.

Why should a hunter hire a guide, as opposed to being self-guided?

Keith Atcheson: There are many reasons to hire a guide. For the most part, hunting on private land is much better than hunting on public land. In today's hectic world most hunters are preoccupied with their own businesses, so it makes a lot of sense to hire an outfitter, hunt private land, and do the trip in less than a week. Our area is inhabited predominantly by mule deer with the occasional whitetail.

Doug Gardner: Here it's mainly for access to lands that are managed for quality and not quantity. You also get a little of the local flavor, and you don't have to worry about getting onto land where you don't have permission to hunt, since that's the guide's responsibility. Here, with scattered public land, there are marked places where you can have access to BLM lands, but it's access mostly to small, almost unhuntable tracts. Usually there's only an entry point that's marked, so you don't know when you go off the tract. An ethical hunter has got to have a huge level of discomfort trying to stay legal while hunting such a place. I guess an unethical hunter just doesn't care if he's trespassing.

Fred Lamphere: By hiring a guide you're buying the guide's knowledge of the land. I'm not opposed to self-guided hunting, and I've had a lot of guys hunt with me one year on a guided hunt and then bring their kid back the next year to hunt unguided on public land. They even call me and ask for information on some of the public places to hunt. I actually encourage that kind of thing. They hunted with me, it was a business deal, and I'm glad that the experience was good enough that they want to hunt mule deer again. If a guy wants to try his hand at public land hunting, more power to him. A guided hunt is a very good way to get started, because you learn something about how to hunt mule deer. They won't be in competition with me, anyway, because all of my hunts are on leased private lands. I'm more than happy to give them directions to public lands.

What is your success rate on trophy animals?

Keith Atcheson: We have had nearly 100 percent success on nice bucks that run 20–25 inches wide with four to five points on each side. Most of our bucks have good mass, great capes, and excellent body coloration. These are some pretty stout deer.

Doug Gardner: Over the years, about 90 percent of our hunters have killed a deer. That doesn't mean they all got the deer of a lifetime, but the vast majority of them come back to hunt again. The people who don't kill a deer are usually looking for a really special deer, a 180-inch buck or so, and that's hard to find. If you're expecting a deer like that, you've got to be prepared to go home without firing your rifle. An old deer of any size and configuration is a trophy to me, and I love it when a guy spends four days looking for that dream buck and then spends the last day looking for a really old buck, regardless of how it scores. That's a real trophy, too, because that deer did everything right to reach 180, except that it didn't have the genetics to make the grade.

Fred Lamphere: I have a lot of repeat hunters, and I'd put my success in the 90 percent range. In my opinion, if the hunter books a hunt and then comes back again, it was successful. I try to judge what a hunter is looking for, and it's different things to different people. If a guy has never shot a mule deer, a mature buck that scores 165 is a fine trophy. I'd say that just about all our hunters have the opportunity to take a buck like that, but some have killed good mule deer before and want to hold out for something special.

A fine high-plains muley taken with Fred Lamphere. (Photo courtesy Fred Lamphere)

Describe your usual hunting method and any common variations.

Keith Atcheson: Most of our hunting is done by spot-and-stalk, and we sometimes leave the ranch house on foot, but most times we begin the hunt by vehicle. Most of the hunting is in the mornings and afternoons, when the deer are active. We also have the luxury of a very long hunting season in Montana that generally runs from the last week of October into the last week of November. Montana is one of the few states that allows mule deer hunting during the rut.

Doug Gardner: Our hunting method changes some as the season progresses, because the animal changes. They're a completely different animal when they're in velvet from the hard-antlered deer of later in the season. Basically, we try to get out early, get on a high point, and do a lot of glassing. If we can't find anything, we may walk some and glass some more, or get in the vehicle and move up another ranch road and take a look from a different high place. When the rifle season opens, the

Another fine high-plains muley. (Photo courtesy Fred Lamphere)

bucks are still in bachelor groups, but when the rut starts they break up for breeding and our tactics have to change.

Fred Lamphere: All our hunts are spot and stalk, even when we're hunting antelope and whitetails. Often we've found the animal well ahead of time, and sometimes I even have photos. Preseason scouting starts in late spring and continues until the season starts.

Do you use any special techniques, such as rattling, grunting, or doe-in-heat lure?

Keith Atcheson: Almost all our hunting is spot and stalk. We haven't found it necessary to use any of the techniques you mention.

Doug Gardner: We use some rattling or grunting to stop a deer or make it feel comfortable with some unnatural noise we've made. I've rattled up a lot of young mule deer, but I've never brought in a good trophy mule deer, and I don't know why that's so. I personally use a coyote call on which I can change the pitch. If you make a good setup to call a coyote, you're very likely to make a deer stand up when you call. We enter one of our big cedar canyons, get where we can see well, and we call just to see what's there. It's surprising how often the deer will come right to us. Sometimes a coyote will come and we'll harvest it! You don't want to overuse that technique, but it's sure nice when a good buck comes to a varmint call, and a lot of times they will, especially during the rut.

Fred Lamphere: No, it's just far too open where our mule deer live. We do use some rattling down in the river bottoms hunting whitetails, but it just isn't feasible on mule deer.

How do you hunt differently when with a client/hunter, as opposed to when hunting alone (for yourself)?

Keith Atcheson: I really don't hunt any differently with a client. I always try to guide a client as if I were doing the hunting myself. That works in favor of us both.

Doug Gardner: It's been tough for me to do any hunting with the schedule we keep. I am also a big advocate of youth hunting, so anytime a hunt is over early and I've got an extra day, I go into town and pick up a kid from school to take hunting. I pick the kids that don't have an opportunity on their own place. Sometimes we go after a cow elk, or else we go for one of those old, low-scoring bucks that are really great trophies anyway. I get a release signed by the parents that I can pick up their kid whenever I want and take them hunting. That's on file in the school office. They're allowed to leave school for the hunt, and when I walk in there and call for them, you can't believe how excited they get. It doesn't do any good just to set a date, because I can never know when I'll have time. I do try to call and let them know it's a possibility for the next week, though, so they won't be completely unprepared. Because I do that hunting program with kids I haven't personally harvested a buck in a long time, but I've sure made friends with a lot of kids over the years.

Great Montana muley by Keith Atcheson. (Photo courtesy Keith Atcheson)

Fred Lamphere: I shot the two best mule deer in my life two and three years ago. When hunting alone I push myself harder and take longer hikes. If I know there's a good buck in a place, I'll walk five miles to get in where he lives and take him on his own playing field. Not all hunters can make a trek like that.

What time of season offers the best hunting in your area (and the highest possibility of success on trophy animals)?

Keith Atcheson: We have a high success rate, so the season isn't that important. The rut is always nice, because the animals are more visible.

Doug Gardner: Here it really doesn't matter. You just have to adjust to differing conditions. Most people either want to hunt the rut, when the deer are less wary, or they want to hunt on opening day before someone else has a chance to kill that big buck. But it works everywhere in between, too.

Fred Lamphere: We have a five-week season in Montana, and in Wyoming we have the whole month of November. In South Dakota it's shorter, starting the second Saturday in November and running until the Sunday after Thanksgiving. I'm going to say that November 5 to 15 is the prime time for the rut. You've got an awful lot of activity then, and you're going to see bucks you've never seen before.

How much does weather influence the hunting success in your area?

Keith Atcheson: Weather in our area definitely has an effect, since snowfall will push game out of the mountains and into the valleys and agricultural fields below, thus making them more accessible.

Putting the final stalk on a muley on the high plains can be a slow, painstaking affair.

The author's high plains muley taken 25 years ago in eastern Wyoming.

Doug Gardner: Rain is probably the worst, because it makes ranch roads muddy, and one thing we will not do is put muddy tracks on a ranch we're leasing. That severely limits mobility, and with the size of these ranches, we have to use vehicles for access. For example, one of our ranches is twenty-five miles from the river boundary to the far edge of the property. Can you imagine having to walk and hunt all that? If we tried to use horses it would be almost impossible because every guide would need a horse trailer and horses. It would be incredibly cumbersome. Visibility can be a problem when we have snow, but at least we can get around. Cold weather doesn't hurt us because we can dress appropriately. Moon phase has some influence, but we know where the deer are located and the country isn't so thick that we can't find them.

Fred Lamphere: It's a big factor. If we have harsh weather, our big buck kill goes way up. Bad weather just pulls them out of those hiding holes and out onto the flats. It takes tough weather to do that. I won't say I like cold and snowy weather, but it sure augments our success! There are a few days when you just can't hunt. But usually you can, and the rougher the weather, the better the success.

How much do weather and time of season influence where and how you hunt in your area?

Keith Atcheson: In general, we can tell whether the game is still in the higher elevations or has dropped down lower. Sometimes many deer that we have never seen before show up in mid-November. We have a wintering area for a lot of game that comes from miles away.

Doug Gardner: If it's been raining, we may hunt off a county road where we can walk in a couple of miles. Or we might change our hunt to another ranch where it didn't rain as much. We also have some places we can go regardless of the rain, and we reserve those for wet weather.

Fred Lamphere: We've got some places we can't hunt if it's really wet, because I've got to work with these ranchers year-round and I can't just go driving around tearing their roads to pieces. Weather influences where we hunt in that way more than any other. But we've got a saying here in South Dakota, that it doesn't matter how wet it is, we're only ten days from a drought. Since 1997 we haven't had a really bad winter, so we've been fortunate. I've never had anyone go home "weathered out," unable to get out and hunt at all because of the weather.

What can a self-guided hunter do to maximize his chances of taking a good mule deer buck on his own?

Keith Atcheson: Self-guided mule deer hunting is a very real possibility for those who choose to do it or can't afford a guide. Seek out places that are well-known mule deer habitat. Read current magazines or even call some of the more knowledgeable writers. They may be more accessible than you think! Buy some good topographical maps of the area you plan to hunt and study both land ownership and terrain. Call local biologists and ask for suggestions. Play the part of "just a common guy" looking for advice on where to go with your kids and father. Look into license availability and whether there are guaranteed licenses or drawings. Find the places that have produced good to exceptional bucks in the past. Then if possible go there in the summer and do some prescouting for a week before the season. Knock on some ranch house doors and ask for permission. Get hold of the fish and game departments and ask if they have a public access hunting program like Montana's highly successful Block Management Program and get on the schedule early. Finding a good place to hunt mule deer in the West is pretty easy. All it takes is a bit of diligence.

Doug Gardner: There are three things a hunter will need: patience, good optics, and the ability to take advantage of the opportunity when it comes. If a self-guided hunter wants to kill nothing less than a good, mature mule deer buck, he's going to have to accept that it's a challenge of the first order. If he's able to do it and then make the shot when it presents, he's got himself a real trophy!

Fred Lamphere: I can't say it enough: Spend plenty of time behind the binoculars. Study the area thoroughly. Don't hesitate to call a guide or outfitter in the area where you want to hunt and get their take on some public land areas. In South Dakota we can't guide paying clients on public land, so it's not competition for us at all. You need to talk to as many local people as you can. If you're coming from back East to hunt South Dakota's public lands, bring the family out for a vacation in August and do some looking around. You shouldn't expect a whole lot out of the first year of doing that, but the better you get to know an area and the more time you invest, the more competent you become and the better your chances.

HUNTING IN THE DESERT SOUTHWEST FOR MULE DEER

Describe your home guiding area for mule deer.

Thomas Brunson: Nevada can best be described as diverse. Two of our units are very high wilderness, more like Wyoming and Utah, and they grow completely different deer from some of our southern units. There are only twenty miles between the two, but the difference in terrain and deer is vast. Down south it's more like southern Utah and Arizona, where there's lots of bitterbrush, piñon-juniper, and rimrock formations. In the north it's typical high country with lots of aspen, mountain mahogany, and sagebrush. The deer down south are more atypical, with lots of extra points and more mass, while the deer in the north have smaller bodies and are more typical, with wide racks but not as much mass. I think some of this is the result of the different minerals available to them.

Troy Justensen: It's really varied here in Utah, everything from typical high desert to alpine terrain, even oak brush and aspen. Probably the most unusual area is the Paunsaugunt, down in the southern part of the state. It's got a phenomenal history of producing giant deer, and the beauty of that red rock and sand country, with its piñon-juniper vegetation, is really special; also, there are a lot of Indian artifacts in the Paunsaugunt. In November, hunting with a muzzleloader, you cover a lot of country because the mule deer herd there migrates, and you can go a long time without seeing much. When you find them, though, you see a lot of them.

Jess Rankin: In Texas we've got some ranches leased that are almost tabletop flat and have different degrees of thick brush. We hunt them primarily out of vehicles. We have the hunter and guide up top in the high seat. Sometimes we shoot the deer from

Great Nevada scenery characterizes a mule deer hunt in that state. (Photo courtesy Thomas Brunson)

the high seat, especially if we're working with a handicapped hunter, but more typically we spot the deer and get down and do a stalk. On those hunts we stay in a nearby motel and drive back and forth every day. We kill some muleys that have really big bodies there. In New Mexico we do two different hunts. One is in south-central New Mexico, where it's really easy to draw a mule deer tag. It's a lot like elk territory, and there are many tall ponderosa pines and piñon-juniper. The hunt is a lot like hunting elk, in fact, although the terrain is much milder than most elk habitat. I also do a hunt up in the northwest corner of the state where only a limited number of people can draw a tag; it's typical rimrock country with deep canyons. There you do a lot of walking and don't see many deer, but there are some real monsters to be had.

What are some distinctions that set it apart?

Thomas Brunson: As I said before, there are actually two very different hunting habitats in Nevada, and they're pretty

Packing it out from remote country is a chore, whether one uses rifle or bow. (Photo courtesy Thomas Brunson)

close together. Also, the excellent game management we have here sets us apart from many other states.

Troy Justensen: All of Utah is limited entry on permits, so the pressure is limited on the animals. Utah has a history of producing some fine mule deer, and that's especially true of the Paunsaugunt area.

Jess Rankin: That draw area is typical of a lot of Western mule deer country, and so is the other New Mexico hunt, so there isn't anything really distinctive. The whole state is wide open country that's ideal for glassing, while down in Texas it's more a vehicle hunt.

Why should a hunter hire a guide, as opposed to being self-guided?

Thomas Brunson: When a person doesn't have the time to do the necessary scouting, they need to hire a guide. One of

A great bow kill in the velvet by Thomas Brunson in Nevada. (Photo courtesy Thomas Brunson)

the primary services I offer is preseason scouting. There are a lot of hunters I guide who are really experienced, and they don't need me to tell them how to hunt mule deer. They could do it on their own if they had the time to do the necessary scouting. They need me, though, to take them where the animals are.

Troy Justensen: It boils down to your expectations for the hunt. If you've got the time and ability to scout effectively, you can do it on your own. If you're lacking either of those commodities, you should hire someone who's been in that country a lot and knows the habits of mule deer. In a lot of the best hunting areas, it takes years of experience to learn what the deer do and how they react to varying hunting pressures and conditions. You increase your odds of finding the buck you want by hiring a guide.

Jess Rankin: In New Mexico, it increases your chances of drawing a tag a tremendous amount if you're in the outfitter pool. If you're hunting on your own it's hard to draw a tag in a lot of

Lots of antler on this big boy. (Photo courtesy Jess Rankin)

areas. If you hire the right outfitter, the guide will know the area, the deer, and where those deer go when they're pressured. It takes a long time to learn such things on your own. Additionally, you can simply show up with your rifle and sleeping bag and not have to worry about setting up camp, cooking, and the like. The reason we hunt is to enjoy ourselves, and it's not much of a vacation when you hunt hard all day and have to come in and cook supper. It's a big time saver, too, because a self-guided hunter would have to come out at least a week early to learn the country to have any kind of chance at a successful hunt.

What is your success rate on trophy animals?

Thomas Brunson: On true trophy animals, and I'm talking about meeting the hunter's expectations, it's probably about 70 percent. Most people who hunt with me are looking for something special.

Troy Justensen: It depends how you want to define a trophy. If you define success as taking an animal, I'd say we're in the

Nice buck from West Texas/New Mexico. (Photo courtesy Jess Rankin)

range of 80 to 85 percent. Some of my hunters are looking for a specific animal, say a Boone and Crockett typical, and we don't shoot unless we see one. That lowers the success rate a bit, but we like to take that type of hunter, too.

Jess Rankin: In the Texas Panhandle it's nearly 100 percent; on the south-central New Mexico hunt it's about 70 percent; and on the hard-to-draw hunt in northwestern New Mexico it's probably more like 50 percent. It's lowest there because I book only experienced deer hunters who want a really big mule deer. Also, some hunters can't hit a running deer, and that doesn't help the success rate.

Describe your usual hunting method and any common variations.

Thomas Brunson: I like to get up high and glass an area where I've found a big buck during preseason scouting. From there it's pretty much patience and intensive glassing. We then plan a stalk to get as close as we can before we attempt a shot.

Troy Justensen: The West is wide open, so we spend a lot of time sitting behind optics. Depending on the time of year, what kind of hunt it is, and what the animals are doing, we might do different things. Down in the Paunsaugunt, where the country is lower and there's a lot of sand, a fresh rain will make tracks stand out. There you can follow a deer until you spot him. It's not like that in other places, where the ground is so hard and rocky that tracking is impossible. Sonora is supposed to be the place where that technique is used, but in my experience it works better right here in Utah. If the year is really dry and the animals are hitting water holes regularly, we'll spend some time sitting over the water and waiting. But by far most of our hunting is spot-and-stalk. We let our optics do the walking most of the time.

Jess Rankin: The two New Mexico hunts are very similar. You get up in the morning and have breakfast, and then you drive to the place where you're going to hunt. You then get out and walk to a glassing place, and after you check things out you walk to another and glass some more. You might do a little ambush work over water holes late in the evening. On our Texas hunts we drive and glass all day, though occasionally we'll make a walk in suitable terrain. The thing I like about that hunt is you usually have time to look the deer over better than here in New Mexico, where so often they're on the move when you see them.

Do you use any special techniques, such as rattling, grunting, or doe-in-heat lure?

Thomas Brunson: I've always wanted to try rattling, but very few of our hunts take place during the rut, so the opportunity isn't there. Sometimes we'll try a drive if it's really slow and there's a full moon, especially if we're certain that a buck is in a particular area. We haven't had much success with that method, though, I must admit. We may see them, but it's tough to kill them. Also, when you disturb an area like that and push a buck out, you're likely never to see him again.

Ask the Mule Deer Guides

Troy Justensen: We've tried rattling with limited success. The most outstanding special technique we use is in the Paunsaugunt, where we can cut a fresh track and follow the deer indefinitely, if conditions are right. It takes really sandy conditions, and in most parts of Utah the technique won't work.

Jess Rankin: No, we don't use any of those techniques.

How do you hunt differently when with a client/hunter, as opposed to when hunting alone (for yourself)?

Thomas Brunson: When I hunt alone, I'm more inclined to try a new spot and do a little exploring. I typically hunt harder, too, and I love to backpack, which most clients either can't do or don't want to do. I like it as remote and as tough as it can get.

Troy Justensen: I don't get much chance to hunt on my own. I get to do everything but pull the trigger, though. I don't think I'd do much differently.

Jess Rankin: It's a whole different deal. The first thing you've got to do as a guide is to figure out the limitations of your hunter. It's a whole lot easier to go out and kill a big deer on my own than it is to guide someone to a big deer, even a good hunter. You've got to study and know your hunter in order to guide him, but you already know yourself.

What time of season offers the best hunting in your area (and the highest possibility of success on trophy animals)?

Thomas Brunson: I think the September muzzleloader hunt is one of the very best. The bucks have just shed their velvet, and they're still pretty much where they've been all summer. As far as seeing huge mule deer, if you can get a chance to hunt them while they're in velvet, that's the time, because they're always right where you found them in the summer.

Troy Justensen: It all depends on the area you're hunting. Utah has a program known as the Cooperative Wildlife Management Unit (CWMU) for private lands, and they have some very lenient seasons that start early, when the bucks are

How much convincing would your guide need to do to get you to shoot this fine buck? (Photo courtesy Troy Justensen)

still in velvet and still out in the open. It's a great time to hunt big mule deer, and you can use a modern rifle. Toward the end of October and the first of November the rut starts, and if you use a muzzleloader there are some really great opportunities. Most of the draw seasons don't allow for hunting with a modern rifle when the bucks are in velvet or during the rut, but you can use one on a CWMU hunt.

Jess Rankin: It's not even a factor. Here in New Mexico we have a five-day season only. In Texas it's a nine-day season, which is centered on Thanksgiving Day.

How much does weather influence the hunting success in your area?

Thomas Brunson: During the rifle season it can be a big factor in some units. If we get weather in some of our southern units the deer start moving toward their winter range, and the transition from summer range to winter range can be as much

Thomas Brunson likes to involve the whole family in deer hunting. (Photo courtesy Thomas Brunson)

as forty miles. The migration takes them through some really thick piñon-juniper country, and it becomes a real hit-or-miss proposition. All our scouting sort of goes out the window, and we just start hitting the transition zones and hoping for the best. The hunting gets better the last week or so of our rifle hunts as the pre-rut starts to kick in and we start seeing bucks coming out to look for does.

Troy Justensen: Snow is a big plus if it comes early, because it forces mature bucks out of the timber up high and into more open country lower down. Cooler weather always helps. Really warm conditions push the deer into the shade, and we don't see as many deer.

Jess Rankin: Weather doesn't affect us much in the Texas Panhandle. In the other areas it can certainly affect the hunt, but it doesn't ever change the way we hunt.

How much do weather and time of season influence where and how you hunt in your area?

Thomas Brunson: They don't change our hunting pattern a lot, but they can certainly make a difference to our success. As I said, when the deer get on the move because of weather, previous scouting is negated and it becomes a guessing game. Early bad weather also sends the bucks into rutting behavior early, and that can help us, even if the does aren't in heat.

Troy Justensen: In a lot of areas you don't have any backup plan, so you've just got to get right in there and keep hunting. When it's hot or the deer have gone nocturnal, you can try to push a deer and get it to move, but you've got only a split second in which to make a decision whether to shoot. If you're trophy hunting that's not an ideal picture, because you like some time to look over the animal.

Jess Rankin: We don't do anything differently because of the weather. Our season is so short that we can't afford to stay out of the field because of weather, even if it's not ideal. Our weather is pretty constant most of the time, though.

What can a self-guided hunter do to maximize his chances of taking a good mule deer buck?

Thomas Brunson: Scouting is paramount, and a self-guided hunter should make it a huge priority. My bread and butter are in the preseason scouting I do, and if you don't do it, your chances are certainly lower.

Troy Justensen: A self-guided hunter is going to need to spend some time familiarizing himself with the unit he'll be hunting, and also do as much scouting as possible. When to scout depends in great part on when your hunt will take place, because if you scout some of these areas in August and find deer, they won't be there if you're hunting the rut or pre-rut. If you're hunting the regular rifle season, a better plan is to discover the habits of the deer in your particular hunting area, such as where they migrate to, and use that information to hunt intelligently.

Ask the Mule Deer Guides

Jess Rankin: There are several things that are important. If he's going to be hunting New Mexico, the self-guided hunter needs to study the drawing odds and harvest statistics, and probably talk to the area biologist about the quality of deer in the area he wants to hunt. He will need to bring good optics, both binoculars and a spotting scope, and know how to use them. I'd re-emphasize that he needs to be able to shoot a moving deer, too. You can tell I've had problems with Eastern hunters trying to kill mule deer on the move.

Chapter 9

HUNTING IN THE CANADIAN WEST FOR MULE DEER

Describe your home guiding area for mule deer.

Bowen Dolhan: We're in northern agricultural areas where a small field is a half-mile by a half-mile. Some are much bigger: a couple of miles wide and deep. These fields back onto huge tracts of forest land with lots of drainages that are tributaries to the Peace River of northern Alberta. We're north of Grande Prairie, Alberta, in the heart of the Peace River country.

Harry Leuenberger: It's rugged mountain terrain that goes up to around nine thousand feet, and our base camp sits at four thousand feet, so we start out from there. The best part is that our mule deer are a migrating herd, and they move down as snow sets in. We've got gorgeous high mountain scenery all around, so it's a really special place.

Nick Frederick: Our home range for mule deer hunting is in east-central Alberta. Our hometown is Coronation, Alberta. We hunt five wildlife management units that total about four million acres. Where we are located is the official division between the Parkland and the Prairie regions of Alberta. The area is privately held farmland with some government grazing leases scattered throughout. The primary crops grown in the area are canola seed, barley, wheat, and peas. Throughout this cropland are stands of aspens along the famous Battle River. The grasslands, which are used mostly for cattle grazing, are made up of native grass with patches of silver willow, which the mule deer love to inhabit. Most of the area is open country, and to the untrained eye it might not look like very good mule deer country. However, to the experienced eye it is obviously a playground for these deer.

Bowen Dolhan's terrific Peace River buck. (Photo courtesy Bowen Dolhan)

What are some distinctions that set it apart?

Bowen Dolhan: Here we have lots of feed for deer, really an endless supply, because of ongoing agriculture. The fields that back onto endless forest land and huge, pristine river drainages are another distinction. That's pretty rare now, because a lot of that kind of land has been developed for other purposes.

Harry Leuenberger: We've got the very best winter range in the eastern Kootenay Mountains, and that's a real plus for our deer. For one thing, there are no cattle at all on that winter range, and the migration routes have good browse all along. Our deer winter well most of the time and are set to survive and grow monstrous antlers for the next hunting season. We also do the best predator control the law allows, with hunts for cougar, wolf, and coyotes. That helps both fawn and adult mule deer survival.

Nick Frederick: The area is on a draw for resident hunters and they acquire a tag on average every three or four years. That gives our bucks ample time to grow up and become mature.

Hunting in the Canadian West for Mule Deer

Nonresident hunters booked with a licensed outfitter do not need to draw a tag, as outfitters own allocations that allow for a restricted number of nonresident hunters each year in each management unit. We are fortunate to be able to hunt the mule deer rut, which runs approximately all the month of November. This gives the hunter a great advantage over hunting other regions that do not allow rifle hunting during the rut. Another distinction is that our whitetail area overlaps our mule deer area in the northern part, so we have the advantage of offering world-class whitetail hunting along with our mule deer hunts.

Why should a hunter hire a guide, as opposed to being self-guided?

Bowen Dolhan: For one thing, there's the time factor. Most hunters don't have the time to do the endless days of scouting that are required to find a real monster buck, and they don't have access to the places that can consistently produce trophy animals. The knowledge that the guide or outfitter has would take years for the average hunter even to approach, so hiring a guide is a recipe for a better chance of success.

Harry Leuenberger: Your success rate is so much better with a guide. It would take the average hunter many years to acquire the experience we have with our area, so naturally the guided hunter is much better off. Another reason is that we've got the right equipment, whether it's horses or whatever.

Nick Frederick: Experience counts, and by hiring a guide you increase your odds tenfold. Guides have experience in the area and permission to hunt, so you don't waste valuable time when you could be out hunting. It could not be any simpler. Our firm has access to more than two hundred private ranches in our hunting area.

What is your success rate on trophy animals?

Bowen Dolhan: That depends on your definition of a trophy animal. If it's one the hunter is happy with, our success rate runs

80 to 90 percent, probably closer to 90. A trophy comes from that tiny 1 percent of the mule deer population that has the age and genetics to achieve uncommonly large antlers.

Harry Leuenberger: First you've got to define what constitutes a trophy. For a twelve-year-old kid from Pennsylvania, a nice typical 4x4 muley that scores 140 is an awesome trophy. I point this out to emphasize that a trophy is in the eye of the beholder. But our success rate on true trophy animals is about 75 percent. I have to assume that if a hunter pulls the trigger, he's happy with the animal he's taking.

Nick Frederick: Our success on trophy mule deer runs anywhere from 80 to 95 percent, depending on the year. A trophy, though, is in the eye of the hunter. We consider a trophy mule deer one that satisfies the client to the point that the cape and antlers go home for mounting. The minimum score for bucks we like to harvest is 165 gross, but we take bucks over 190 every year. If the biggest buck you have taken is a 150 mule deer, we advise you not to come on one of our hunts and pass 170-class bucks seeking a giant that will score over 200. It's wise to work your way up the ladder. Once you have killed a 180+ buck you can continue harvesting that class of deer because ground expansion can occur, though it isn't as common as ground shrinkage.

Describe your usual hunting method and any common variations.

Bowen Dolhan: It would vary throughout the season. Early in the season I scout the fields, and we are looking at fields that have wheat in them that is three or four feet tall. Until you go there a dozen times, you don't have any idea what's living there. There are places I know that consistently have trophy bucks, but it takes time to see them. Most of the techniques we use involve some variation of spot-and-stalk. The deer we want will often bed down in standing wheat or canola fields, or whatever is growing, and we wait for them to do that. We've scouted them enough that we usually know how many hours they'll bed

Snow camouflage certainly helps when hunting late-season bucks in Canada. (Photo courtesy Nick Frederick)

down for, and when they'll stand up again. The way we approach them usually involves a lot of belly crawling or removing shoes and stalking. When we get them to stand up, we use shooting sticks to get the hunter a shot from as close as possible.

Harry Leuenberger: I could really go into detail on this question. We leave camp early in the morning, typically on horseback but sometimes in a pickup or on a quad, depending on weather conditions and time of year. We hunt pretty much all day, finding high vantage points so we can glass and really check out the terrain. We know the areas the deer are coming through, so we get in the right spot to glass and we cover a whole basin. A basin can look completely empty, but all of a sudden there's a deer, and then there are others, and you wonder where they all came from.

Nick Frederick: Most of our hunting days begin by leaving the lodge in a pickup truck. We go to a good vantage point to glass for bucks. Once a good buck is spotted a plan is put

This great Peace River buck is wide with long tines. (Photo courtesy Nick Frederick)

into place to try to take him. Where spotting from afar is not possible, we sometimes walk river bottoms or ridges trying to jump a buck out of its bed. That type of hunting is better done from late morning onward, as the deer are already bedded. Some of the other county can be hunted from the vehicle by traveling slowly through pastures and fields. Our most successful methods involve walking and stalking. While hunting with clients you must keep them busy all day, because they didn't travel such a long distance to sit in a lodge when the deer are not moving.

Do you use any special techniques, such as rattling, grunting, or doe-in-heat lure?

Bowen Dolhan: None of those have worked for me, but I do use a special technique known as "bumping deer." I'll circle around behind the deer as far as half a mile, with the hunter set up on an escape route. Usually before the season I do this same routine when I find a good buck bedded in a field, and I observe where the deer departs, never spooking the buck but just getting him uncomfortable enough to leave the field. That way I know his preferred exit route, and I can set the hunter up in good position to take him. If we come across him again while hunting, I put the hunter on that escape route and I start from a long ways off, almost like a farmer herding cows. I move toward the buck so slowly that he eventually gets up and walks away. You can't push too hard when you do this, or else the buck will spook and go places you've not seen him go before—and fast! You've got to be sure he simply gets up and walks out of the field. We take a lot of bucks that way.

Harry Leuenberger: Most of our hunting is straightforward looking and glassing until we find the right buck, and then planning a stalk to get close enough for a shot. For the past couple of years we've used a fawn bleat call that really brings in the does, and if there's a buck handy he'll likely come after them. It's actually worked very well several times, and we've used it to take some outstanding bucks.

Nick Frederick: When we deviate from any of our usual hunting methods, the most common technique is a fawn distress call. We have taken big bucks by calling a doe out of a brush patch or just back over the hill toward us. The doe comes to see what is going on, and the big boys follow.

How do you hunt differently with a client/hunter, as opposed to when hunting alone [for yourself]?

Bowen Dolhan: I do it quite differently. When I'm hunting for myself it's a lot easier and more relaxed. When I take a client out it's to the extreme, with 100 percent effort all the time. I slow the pace down quite a bit when I'm hunting for myself, and I enjoy it even more. When a hunter is paying for your time, you owe him a total effort, and it can be grueling at times.

Harry Leuenberger: If the hunter is in good shape there's absolutely no difference. If he's not in good shape, you just have to take your time and go at his pace.

Ask the Mule Deer Guides

Nick Frederick: I go a lot harder when I hunt alone. Often the client wants to take an afternoon siesta while things are quiet, but when I go by myself I never do that.

What time of season offers the best hunting in your area (and the highest possibility of success on trophy animals)?

Bowen Dolhan: That would be from the opening of rifle season in the middle of September until the beginning of October, when the bucks haven't been harassed at all. Bow season opens August 25 and runs until the opening of rifle season, and that's also a very good time to hunt. Rifle season runs all the way to the end of November, so it's a good, long season that allows you to hunt the rut, which is another great time to hunt. During the rut, bucks you've never even seen show up. The hardest time is the last three weeks of October, when the bucks are in pre-rut mode.

Harry Leuenberger: Our season runs from September 1 to September 9 for archery hunting. Rifle season opens September 10 and runs to November 15. Anytime from October 25 to November 15 is best for hunting, because that's the rut. Of course, a lot depends on snow conditions. Deer are coming out of the mountains and migrating to their winter ranges, and that's when the best bucks are generally taken.

Nick Frederick: The best time to hunt for mule deer in our area is the month of November. The rut is on then, and each week has some kind of advantage over the other weeks. The first part of the month is opening week, so things are good. In the middle of the month the rut is peaking, though toward the end of the month the bucks tend to go back to their normal feeding practices and get a little harder to spot.

How much does the weather influence hunting success in your area?

Bowen Dolhan: A lot. Deer movement depends on the weather, and the visibility of bucks depends on their moving. If

Plenty of extra points on this terrific Alberta muley. (Photo courtesy Nick Frederick)

those bucks aren't moving, they can be tough to find. And if they aren't out and about, it's usually because of the weather. Rain doesn't keep them from moving, but it makes them head for the bushes where they're very hard to see. That's not a big deal, though, if you know where to go for the best chances of seeing them. During a prestorm period, you just don't see many deer at all.

Harry Leuenberger: Weather is a big factor, a tremendous one, in fact. If there is rain or fog in November, instead of snow, you can't hunt because you can't glass. You have to be lucky and set up on a migration route in order to be successful under those circumstances. Heavy snow brings the deer down into the winter range more quickly, so it can be an advantage. In an average year, our snows start about the middle of October and increase after that.

Nick Frederick: Weather does play a role in our area in one regard, and that's when there's fog. We generally get fog one or two days a year, and with the fog usually comes a very slow

165

deer hunt. Fortunately it passes quickly, but the fog can be very thick in our part of the province.

How much do weather and time of season influence where and how you hunt in your area?

Bowen Dolhan: Just after a storm, when the deer have been "bushed up" for two or three days and then come back out onto the fields, is a time when they're very skittish. They're used to having plenty of cover in the fields, and after a storm it isn't as high, which makes them really wary. We hold off for several days to let them get accustomed to the new lay of the land before we even try to make a move on them.

Harry Leuenberger: We do have alternative places to hunt if conditions are poor for our usual places and methods. We can head down to the winter range if we get bad rain and fog, or if we've got so much snow in the high country that the horses can't get through. The lower country, which we call the Rocky Ridges, along the Wigwam River, is a great place when conditions in the higher terrain are unhuntable. Most of our hunters carry a whitetail tag, too, and sometimes we can find a great whitetail when we're forced to hunt the lower country, so it's not all bad to hunt the alternative areas.

Nick Frederick: Snow is best for hunting big muley bucks. On a normal year we will get snow the first of November, and it will stay the rest of the year. It's great for tracking, of course, and it greatly enhances our ability to spot movement. I can't say that it changes our basic pattern of hunting, though.

What can a self-guided hunter do to maximize his chances of taking a good mule deer buck?

Bowen Dolhan: Plenty of scouting is required, along with research on what kind of deer have come out of the area. You can't just pull trophy mule deer out of areas that have never produced them before. It takes a lot of homework for a self-guided hunter to be successful on a real trophy mule deer. Of course, here in Alberta nonresidents must have a guide by law, so I'm talking about Alberta residents.

Harry Leuenberger: The self-guided hunter has to do his homework. He's got to hunt smart, keep the wind right, and find a good vantage point to do that essential glassing. Preseason scouting helps, but it's deceptive because you may see good deer in August that won't be there when rifle season opens. For a bow hunter, late August scouting is ideal because the deer will probably be right there when the bow season opens. If you're planning to hunt the rut, scouting in August is pretty much a waste of time.

Nick Frederick: Our provincial laws make it impossible for nonresident hunters to guide themselves here in Alberta. Alberta residents need to do a lot of scouting prior to the season and look for mule deer in areas that have traditionally produced big bucks.

Chapter 10

HUNTING IN MEXICO FOR MULE DEER

Describe your home guiding area for mule deer.

Mick Chapel: In Sonora, most of the ranches we have leased have been prepared as I described earlier, pushing out the brush with a bulldozer and planting a kind of fast-growing grass from Africa. It grows three inches a day when it has water, but a hard frost will kill it. They take a bulldozer with a huge disk harrow behind it and a seed box behind that, and they meander around in that thick brush cutting open areas. They don't take all the brush, but where they do open it up they plant the grass. It's perfect for hunting. I like a ranch that has little knobs scattered around where you can sit and glass for deer.

Eduardo Gomez Jr.: It's a fairly flat area with a few low hills. The main kinds of vegetation are ironwood and paloverde trees of medium height that shield and protect the mule deer. There are a lot of thorny desert plants, such as *uña de gato,* that the hunter should avoid.

David Lopez: The area here has thick desert vegetation with lots of cholla cactus, which is a preferred food of the desert mule deer. Access is controlled so that the deer have opportunity to grow to full maturity. The desert is an interesting place, and its vegetation is unique. It takes a lot of experience to hunt it safely and successfully.

What are some distinctions that set it apart?

Mick Chapel: The sheer size of some of our properties in Sonora is probably a major distinction. Some ranches are sixty-five thousand acres or more, or at least we've put together two or three adjacent ranches that total that much. Some have been

Another great Sonoran buck taken while Brent Sinclair was along. (Photo courtesy Brent Sinclair)

prepared, but some are so thick you can't get around on them. You want it that way so you've got an edge to hunt, where deer are coming and going to and from the grassy areas and brush.

Eduardo Gomez Jr.: Sonora is almost entirely private land, so we lease large ranches with plenty of food and cover for the deer. We guard it from poaching and protect the deer and their habitat so the hunting remains good.

David Lopez: There is really good cover, which gives the mule deer a sense of security that is lacking in more open areas. Our area also has excellent food sources, so the deer can grow big.

Why should a hunter hire a guide, as opposed to being self-guided?

Mick Chapel: In Mexico you really don't have a choice, because you must have a guide and a place to hunt. Apart from that technicality, there are two good reasons: inexperience hunting desert mule deer on your own and access to good hunting territory. If you draw a tag in a good area out West, you can come out and have good success on your own if you're a seasoned hunter. You've got to be able to look at the country and assess its potential, though.

Eduardo Gomez Jr.: Because it is better to hunt with someone who knows the area. That not only gives one a better chance at taking a good desert mule deer but also increases safety and decreases risks.

David Lopez: The desert can be a very dangerous place, and getting lost can mean dying. A good guide will keep you from getting lost and also knows where to hunt, so you have the best chance of success.

What is your success rate on trophy animals?

Mick Chapel: In Mexico it's around 70 percent.

Eduardo Gomez Jr.: Most of the time we run close to 90 percent on trophy mule deer.

David Lopez: My success rate runs about 80 percent on trophy mule deer.

Describe your usual hunting method and any common variations.

Mick Chapel: Let me be clear on one thing: This idea of following a set of tracks until you jump the deer is mostly a lot of bull. I can follow tracks better than most anybody I know, because I spend five months a year following tracks. Down there, though, the ground is so hard and there are so many tracks that it's hopeless. In some places you can do it, but not in most areas in Sonora. Up in northern New Mexico I can follow tracks until I jump the deer. I can even tell when he's going to lie down, because he starts to wander from side to side. I tell my hunter to get ready, and all of a sudden, there he is! We've got it down to an art, but it doesn't work in Sonora because of the incredibly

A superlative buck from Sonora—it's the reason we hunt there! (Photo courtesy Brent Sinclair)

hard soil. There it's mostly glassing from the high points until we see the deer we want.

Eduardo Gomez Jr.: We begin our hunting on 4x4 pickups with high towers, which allows us to move around large areas with great visibility for the hunter. That is also important because it helps us to judge a good buck from the vehicle even if it is far away. We also use hills to glass over the valley and put high towers near water holes.

David Lopez: We leave very early in the morning and drive to an area we've already scouted where we know there's a good buck, so we can be glassing at first light. If we don't see what we're seeking, we start moving around carefully, watching and waiting for our buck to present himself. Sometimes we find a small hill that gives us good visibility, and we may spend up to two hours glassing from there. When we see the buck we want, we try to maneuver into position for a shot.

Do you use any special techniques, such as rattling, grunting, or doe-in-heat lure?

Mick Chapel: No, we don't use any of those. I don't believe mule deer are very likely to come to any kind of call. We do sit over water holes sometimes, because it's extremely dry down there. The deer don't necessarily need to come to water, though, because if you knock down one of those cholla cacti, or any other kind of cactus, water comes out. The deer are able to get their water from what they eat, but if water is available they will sometimes come to it. I don't think they like to come to water, though, because they feel vulnerable there.

Eduardo Gomez Jr.: I've tried all of those several times but with no positive results. The hunter needs to be very lucky to take a big mule deer. I think our standard techniques are much better than those special techniques. We try to set up near where we know there are deer, or else we glass until we see them move.

David Lopez: Our only special technique is preseason scouting and lots of glassing until we find what we're looking for.

How do you hunt differently when with a client/hunter, as opposed to when hunting alone (for yourself)?

Mick Chapel: I don't hunt differently; I hunt almost exactly the same. I glass awhile and move, then glass more and move again. Some people like to sit in one place and glass for hours, and that works fine, too. The big thing is to keep glassing, because the deer definitely get up and move in the middle of the day.

Eduardo Gomez Jr.: I don't hunt for myself anymore. I enjoy much more doing the hunt with a client.

David Lopez: I do everything just the same.

What time of season offers the best hunting in your area (and the highest possibility of success on trophy animals)?

Mick Chapel: You need to go to Sonora in late December or early January. If you don't hunt then, you're certain to hunt on a

A fabulous Sonora buck taken by Sonora Adventures. (Photo courtesy Eduardo Gomez)

ranch that's already been hunted. In Mexico, it's all interchangeable, too. If a guy gets twelve mule deer tags on his ranch and you buy them all, nobody else hunts the place, so you're kidding yourself. They can buy those tags from anybody who's got them, whether it's from an adjacent ranch or one three hundred miles away. So my advice is to go early. That's the heart of the rut, too.

Eduardo Gomez Jr.: The best hunting is in January during the dark of the moon. I've noticed that the rut seems to peak between the ninth and the twentieth of January.

David Lopez: The very best time to hunt in Sonora is in January, because mule deer bucks are rutting and thus are moving around more. Your best chance at a big buck in Sonora is during the January rut.

How much does weather influence the hunting success in your area?

Mick Chapel: It's no more or less a factor than anywhere else. It's not a big factor, in any case. One thing that is a big factor, though, is hunting pressure, and big mule deer don't take

Another wonderful Sonora buck. (Photo courtesy Robb Wiley)

to that very well. We had a young kid pass up a huge mule deer at 170 yards. He refused to shoot because one antler had a broken tine. We figured it would gross score around 217. The other hunters in camp gave him a really hard time for passing on that kind of deer, but you know what? We never saw that deer again in three more weeks of hunting.

Eduardo Gomez Jr.: The biggest factor regarding weather is when it becomes unexpectedly warm in January. The bucks stop chasing does and become very difficult to find if the temperature rises.

David Lopez: Cool weather and rain have a very positive effect on hunting in Sonora. Neither is particularly common, but when cool weather moves in the rut really kicks off. Rain is a help because it keeps the air cool, so the deer move a lot. But

Glassing thick brush in Sonora can be a challenge.

it also washes out old tracks and makes following a good buck much easier. If it's warm and dry, the hunt is much harder.

How much do weather and time of season influence where and how you hunt in your area?

Mick Chapel: As I said, in Mexico the most important factor is getting there before anyone else does! The rut in late December and early January is the best time to hunt, but we don't hunt any differently because of weather.

Eduardo Gomez Jr.: They affect us very much. If we don't get our normal cold weather the animals don't move. Warm winters are the worst enemy for us, and rain is even worse: There is water available everywhere, so it is much more difficult to see deer.

Ask the Mule Deer Guides

David Lopez: We move to an area with better visibility when it's hot and dry so we can glass a lot of country. If it's rainy or cold we can get in much closer and try to find the animal we want. Weather can make us move from one area to another to maximize our chances.

What can a self-guided hunter do to maximize his chances of taking a good mule deer buck on his own?

Mick Chapel: As noted, you can't guide yourself in Mexico unless you hook up with some rancher down there and lease his ranch. Then you can guide yourself, if you have the financial means to do that. Just remember, though, that you've got to be very careful in Mexico, because money is first and everything else is secondary. Unless you've got a really good relationship with a Mexican rancher, you're better off letting a seasoned outfitter do the bargaining for you. To hear most Sonoran ranchers tell it, all of them have ranches that have never been hunted!

Eduardo Gomez Jr.: Unless you lease someone's ranch in Sonora, it's not possible to guide yourself to a mule deer there.

David Lopez: In Sonora, a non-Mexican hunter must have a guide unless he's leasing the land for himself. In most cases the hunter needs a guide who has been watching a piece of property for months so he can know exactly what kind of deer are living there. If you have no idea about such things, you might as well just shoot into the darkness. Your chances of success are about the same.

Chapter 11

PARTING SHOTS FROM THE MULE DEER GUIDES

Do you have any unusual mule deer hunting stories to share?

Grant Adkisson: When I was guiding as a very young man, probably still in my teens, I had a fairly novice hunter with me. We had seen a mule deer go into some piñons, and I thought we had a chance to get him. We were trying to get in where we could see the buck when it jumped up and started running off. My hunter made a beautiful running shot, and the buck went down immediately and seemed to be dead. We walked over to the animal and started admiring it, and it really was a fantastic buck. The hunter said he was going to tag the animal right away, so he took his tag out of his pocket. I told him that could wait until after we took some pictures and got the deer field dressed, but he went ahead and placed the tag on the antlers and tied it with a tight knot. Then we got ready to do the chores on the animal.

We had barely turned to start our jobs when the buck jumped up and ran away! We grabbed the gun and took off after it as it disappeared over a little hill. Before we could get to where we might see another glimpse, we heard two shots ring out. We arrived to find a hunter my uncle was guiding standing over my hunter's buck. They had been riding by on horses when our buck appeared out of nowhere, so the guy got off his horse and shot it dead. They were standing by the buck talking when we came running up, and my hunter blurted out, "That's my buck!"

The other hunter said, "I don't think so. I just shot it."

My hunter replied, "It's my buck! There's my tag!"

The other hunter looked at the tag and said to my hunter, "Well, if you're man enough to tag a buck before it's shot, I guess it is your buck."

Long tines and plenty of mass on this Alberta buck. (Photo courtesy Grant Adkisson)

Another story involves a hunter I was guiding. We were taking a break and having lunch. Somebody had pushed a buck from some other part of the ranch, and it was suddenly running by us at less than fifty yards' distance. The hunter jumped up, sighted in on the animal, and then began to eject his shells one by one until all seven were lying on the ground. He said, "I can't believe I missed that buck every time."

I told him to look at the pile of unspent shells on the ground. He hadn't even pulled the trigger!

Jeff Chadd: Once I had a guy shoot a buck, and he set his rifle down. We went over to look at the animal, and when we got there the buck jumped up and took off. It was a fiasco. As I ran back to get his rifle, he was just standing there watching that big buck run away. The way that animal went down I thought for sure it was over. The buck was hit hard, but the bullet had gone in high. The deer ran only about a hundred yards and then lay down again. Fortunately, we were able to catch up to it and get in another shot.

Robb Wiley: One of my clients had extremely high expectations. He told me that he wouldn't shoot a deer scoring under 200 inches. I did a lot of preseason scouting and located a deer that would exceed even that high standard. There aren't a lot of deer like that, so we had to concentrate on the area where I'd seen that buck. I spent the entire hunt glassing from one single vantage point because from there I could see all the country where the big buck lived.

On the first day the hunter was enthusiastic, on the second day he was discouraged, and on the third day he was beginning to become irritated. By the fourth day he had become angry and told me that I had wasted his time, I had wasted his money, and I was taking advantage of him because there were no deer in that country. He pointed out that all he had seen were a couple of does. I kept telling him to be patient because we were there for a specific reason. I'd smile and try to work with him as best I could to keep his spirits up, but it was becoming increasingly hard. On the fifth day, he saw the largest mule deer he'd ever seen in his life.

He apologized profusely and has been a return client ever since. He had his chance, but he didn't get that big one. But he did realize that I was doing what it took to give him the chance he wanted.

Keith Atcheson: In the early 1990s I had a hunting camp based out of Sand Springs, Montana. We had three large mobile trailers, one that housed all of our clients and the other two for my young family and our hunting guides. I had about six hunters in camp at the time, including one particular client I'll call "Bob."

Bob had telephoned me only the month before this hunt to inform me he held a valid deer license for that year and wanted to come hunting for mule deer as soon as possible. He explained to me that he did not have long to live, as he had a very severe heart condition and this hunt would most likely be his last. I asked him to describe himself and his condition as I was concerned about fielding this hunt, nor was I certain I had an opening.

He told me he was just over five feet tall and weighed 350 pounds. I asked him about his expectations, and he told me he wanted a 30-inch mule deer or nothing. I explained to him that in twenty years of outfitting we had killed only a couple that even approached that standard, and that there were very few of that width in our area. He asked me if there was any chance at all of getting a deer in that class, and I told him it was in the range of 1 percent. That was all Bob needed, and at the end of the discussion I told him I would look into my schedule to see if I could accommodate him.

I determined that there was an opening available, and I had him come out at the best time. When he arrived, his physical appearance was alarming. There was no way Bob was going to do much walking, so I decided to give him my most experienced guide, a retired rancher from eastern Montana. I figured they would get along well and cover a lot of country by vehicle. By about halfway through the hunt, Bob had already passed on several decent 5x5 mule deer, including one that was maybe 27 inches wide, certainly a trophy buck in our area.

One morning during Bob's hunt, one of the hunters came running over to my trailer and said, "Keith, come quick. We have a water leak in our trailer."

I rushed out the door and over to the client's trailer, and the hunters directed me to the back where the bathroom was located. I stuck my head in the door, and to my dismay I saw the toilet tank and toilet bowl lying in pieces on the floor, with water gushing from the water supply line. I quickly reached down and turned off the water. While I was looking at the mess on the floor and

Plenty of mass in this velvet-covered buck. (Photo courtesy Jeff Chadd)

wondering what had happened, one of the hunters tapped me on the shoulder and told me I should talk to Bob, who had an entrance from his bedroom to that same bathroom.

When I walked into Bob's bedroom, I saw he was wearing only bloodied underwear and was holding a large bath towel, heavily soaked in blood, against his forehead. I said, "Let me take a look at that wound."

He lowered the towel, and there on his forehead was a huge, egg-size bump with a three-inch gash that would need stitches. I asked Bob, who was sitting on the bed shaking his head back and forth, what had happened, but he was too embarrassed to tell me.

I said, "We are going to the hospital as soon as possible."

There was disgust in his voice, but he agreed. He then explained to me that his alarm clock had gone off, so he had gotten out of bed and was walking into the bathroom when he tripped over his hunting boots and fell through the bathroom door, flying headfirst into the toilet bowl. His head literally broke the toilet bowl and tank into pieces. It still amazes me such a thing could happen, but Bob did it.

The nearest hospital was a hundred miles away in Lewistown, Montana, and we were there in an hour and a half. I got him checked into the emergency room, and while he was getting stitched up I went to a hardware store and bought another toilet. Bob got patched up and finished his hunt with us over the next couple of days, passing on a few more deer. He never got the deer of his dreams, but he gave it his best effort. Sadly, he died a month after his mule deer hunt with us.

Doug Gardner: I was hunting with a young fellow from Pennsylvania one cold, windy day. We'd put a long sneak on a good rutting buck that was accompanied by some does. It was about a 170-class buck, a nice muley. We were just getting ready to make the final approach, and I peeked over a boulder and noted that the does were getting extremely nervous. I immediately thought that maybe there was a big cougar in the area that was stirring things up.

The buck was trying to catch up with the does, and they were circling in a crazy way. All of a sudden a much bigger buck appeared out of nowhere—he was the cause of all that commotion! We watched those two bucks have a heck of a fight, and then my hunter shot the better of the two. It was the experience of a lifetime, and the buck of a lifetime, too. It was 30 inches wide with sticker points on both sides, a real trophy. The odds of making a stalk on a really good deer and then getting surprised by the appearance of an even better one have got to be really low. It was quite a thrill, but I'm not sure that the young fellow appreciated it at the time. He's since been back several times to try to get a better deer, and by now I think he does appreciate it.

Fred Lamphere: A coworker of my brother down in Texas, a hardworking guy, really wanted to hunt mule deer. He'd been to western Texas and Colorado, but he had never been successful.

He talked to my brother, and that led him to book a hunt with us in Montana. I picked him up at the Rapid City Airport, and he was eager to get hunting.

He told me right off that he was looking for a mule deer that was fairly wide and with good mass. Before I could tell him that he'd probably have to give up one of those to get the other, he went on to say that he wanted its rack to be nice and tall, too, and to have at least five points on a side. I hadn't said a word at that point, but a lot of things were going through my mind. I finally told him he'd just described the perfect mule deer, and that I hoped we could find him one.

His hunt didn't start until the next day, and he'd landed in Rapid City about noon, so we got to the lodge by 3:30 P.M. I knew the ranch where we were going to hunt, and the season was already in full swing. With all this guy's expectations in the back of my mind, I was thinking how best to enlighten him. I knew from experience that sometimes if the antlers were wide they were also thin, or a buck will be a 4x5 instead of a 5x5, and maybe one tine won't fork on one side. We pulled up to the ranch, and I was going to give him the layout as we watched the sunset and observed the deer as they came out to feed in the nearby alfalfa fields. I also planned to explain where we'd be in the morning, which wasn't too far from the lodge.

All his gear was still in the back of the pickup, and his rifle was in its secure flight case. We were glassing over the alfalfa fields and watching the deer come out of some of the breaks, and I spotted a doe standing in high weeds off to one side at the back of the hayfield. I could see another deer behind it, and I put my binoculars on it. It was a buck. They were maybe 125 yards away, and up came that buck's head with a great set of antlers!

He curled his lip and tried to mount the doe. I did a double-take and looked again. I couldn't believe it, but I was looking at a 28-inch 5x5 mule deer that was over 300 pounds on the hoof, and he was wide, heavy, and tall, with gorgeous dark antlers. I turned to my hunter and said, "Look, I know your hunt doesn't start until tomorrow, and you've got five days to hunt, but the deer you just told me you want is right down there below us."

I pointed out the buck to him, and then we made a mad rush getting his rifle unsecured and getting his cartridges out of his other luggage. That buck was in rut, though, and the only thing that was going to keep him from breeding that doe was getting shot. And that's what we did! The hunt was over before it started, but that hunter left a happy man.

Thomas Brunson: Three years ago I finally had my first chance to chase mule deer for myself using a bow. The hunt was going well, and I was backpacking into some remote country and seeing some great bucks. I chased around a couple of 30-plus-inch nontypicals for a couple of days before deciding that about a thousand feet of shale rock I had to sneak through wasn't going to allow me an opportunity to get within archery range. There was one good basin I hadn't checked out, though, so I loaded up camp and off I went.

A few hours later, with a new camp situated, I was again glassing for bucks. It was midday and there was no activity. All of a sudden while scanning the aspens with my spotting scope I located the largest buck I had ever laid eyes on. After about ten minutes of dancing around and giggling like a little girl, I got a real good look at the buck. It was sporting eleven points on one side and twelve on the other, and I estimated that it would gross score in the low- to mid-230s. Now it was time to get serious.

I sneaked on the buck five times over the next four days, one time closing the distance to about eighty yards before getting pinned down by a two-point and having to crawl out backward for about four hundred yards. Finally, on the morning of the fourth day, an opportunity presented. I was in the aspens before light and was right under the buck with a perfect wind mirroring his movements, waiting until he decided that it was time to make his way to bed.

I was set up on a trail two hundred yards below the buck as it was heading straight toward me. Everything was perfect! The trees were really thick just before the point where the buck would step out, allowing me to draw my bow. The trail was forty yards above me, and I was deadly at that distance. As the buck approached the trees, I drew my bow. But as I came to my anchor point, I realized that something was terribly wrong.

Awesome scenery surrounds the hunt for this Wyoming buck. (Photo courtesy Robb Wiley)

The face mask I was wearing was built like a ski mask that pulls all the way over the head, with two little eye holes cut out of it. Because of the material between the eyes, I was not able to see my pins. Panic and buck fever then set in, and I didn't know what to do. So I just opened my nonshooting eye and tried to line it up, and I let go an arrow. My heart fell into my stomach as I heard the arrow skipping through the rocks. And as if that weren't bad enough, the buck took two jumps and stopped broadside with the trunk of an aspen blocking its face, allowing me another shot. I was so rattled by then, though, that I drew my bow and realized that I had the same problem as before! I had again forgotten about the face mask and now sent another blind arrow smacking through the aspens. I had messed up not only one once-in-a-lifetime shot, but two!

All of this could have been avoided had I just done a little practice with the equipment that I was going to be using in the field. I hope that after you read this it won't happen to you. Another

Incredible length and mass on this velvet-covered Nevada giant. (Photo courtesy Thomas Brunson)

word of caution: I have seen thousands of mule deer bucks and some giant ones, so nobody is immune to buck fever!

Troy Justensen: We had spotted a particular deer we wanted to take, and we knew that it had bedded in a certain clump of trees. Because we knew it was the buck we wanted, I was a little more willing than usual to try to get it up and moving. I set the hunter up in a good spot and circled to drive the buck out. It worked like a charm, which it often doesn't, but that deer ran right by the hunter. I kept waiting for the shooting to start, and sure enough, there was a single shot. I hurried over to the hunter, and he was standing in a pile of unspent ammunition! He said, "I guess I got a little excited."

He'd gotten a little buck fever and had ejected all but one shell without pulling the trigger! However, the really unusual part is that he used that last shot to kill the deer cleanly! And it was a really nice deer.

Jess Rankin: I call this one "Better Lucky Than Good." Several years ago I had a camp of hunters for elk in an area in southwestern New Mexico known for big bulls. Since the last three days of this five-day elk hunt overlapped with the first three days of deer season in the same area, and deer tags were sold over the counter, I had all my elk hunters buy deer tags. This area has produced some excellent desert mule deer and Coues whitetail in the past.

On the fourth afternoon of the hunt a couple of my guides and one hunter were working their way up a big canyon, looking primarily for a bull elk. One of the guides spotted a modest 3x3 mule deer buck standing on a big rock on the opposite side of the canyon. The buck was only about 22 inches wide and not very tall or heavy. Both guides tried to talk the hunter out of shooting the buck, but the hunter was determined to shoot anything with antlers. The guides got the hunter set up for the shot with a solid rest on a backpack that had been laid across a big rock. One of the guides estimated the distance at 350 yards. The hunter fired and hit a couple of feet low, striking the rock the buck was standing on.

At the shot the buck jumped off the rock and a big 4x4 buck that had been bedded down beneath the rock jumped up on top, right where the little buck had been standing. The hunter now realized that the shot was farther than 350 yards, so he shot at the big buck, aiming a couple of feet higher than the first shot. The shot dropped the buck on the spot with a broken back. One of the guides afterward took a GPS reading and found that the distance was 435 yards. The buck was a beautiful 26-inch-wide 4x4 with eye guards that gross scored 187 and change. I'm sure glad my guide underestimated the distance!

Bowen Dolhan: Oh, lots! I don't know where to start! One time we had been hunting a deer that was living on posted land, but every once in a while I would catch him on property that was open—but usually at night. You could tell by watching him, though, that he knew he was in trouble when he was off that property, so he didn't come off very much.

I had a hunter on a ten-day hunt, and we hunted that deer for eight days and never caught him off the posted property. By that time I decided we had nothing to lose, so I talked to the landowner and told him the situation—that we were after only one deer, and so on—and to my surprise he gave us permission to hunt!

We had been able to see the deer bedded in the middle of that property all day long every day, and sure enough when we drove to that field there were dozens of deer about. The one we wanted was bedded in the middle of the field, as usual, and that buck's eyes almost popped out of its head. We could see the wheels turning, and it was clear he knew the game was up. We drove the truck within seventy-five yards of him, and he just lay there because he knew he had nowhere to go that we couldn't follow.

We started contemplating the situation because it was too easy now, and the hunter and I decided we couldn't shoot that buck. The buck finally got up, slowly walked off over a small rise about 150 yards away, and bedded down again. He lay his head and antlers as flat as he could on the ground, as if he were hiding. We just turned around and drove away. The hunter ended up killing a 200-point deer on the very last day in a different place, so he was well rewarded for refusing to take the easy one.

Another time we were after a great buck we knew to be in a wheat field. That year the crops were over four feet tall, and bucks would bed in there all day long without moving so you couldn't see them. They were feeding mostly after dark, making it tough to get a chance for a shot. I finally put my hunter up on a big brush pile so he could see, and I started my bumping technique down at the far end of the field. I had pushed fourteen bucks out of that field, but the big guy just wouldn't move. I was getting so close that I had no choice but to keep on going, and I was even yelling. When he finally stood up, he was less than twenty yards from me! When the hunter looked through his scope, both the buck and I were in his field of view, so he couldn't shoot. He did shoot at the buck as it began to run away, but it was a clean miss. That buck knew the game and wasn't playing!

Harry Leuenberger: I had a hunter on a mountain we call the China Wall. It's a really big mountain with good winter range nearby and lots of mule deer migration. We hiked up and found a 180-class deer with some does, so we put a stalk on him and got up on top of the ridge. Well, the wind changed, the does got our scent, and the buck got up to move away with them. The hunter bellied down and shot at the back of the buck's head just as it was crossing an avalanche slide. That deer went down as though it had been hit with an ax and never even twitched.

As we were congratulating each other on the beautiful deer we'd taken, slapping each other on the back, and so on, the buck started sliding down the avalanche trail. The movement was slow, and it was collecting snow in front of it, so it would stop from time to time. The hunter asked if he should put another shot in it, but I was so sure it was dead that I told him not to bother. All of a sudden the deer kicked a little, and then it started moving down the slide on its back again. It did that a couple of times. The slide disappeared around the corner, and eventually the deer just slid out of sight.

We started down, figuring we had a dead deer just around the bend. When we got over to the slide, there was zero blood. We went to the spot where the deer had disappeared around the corner just in time to see that big buck bouncing away through some alders across the canyon! The only thing I can figure is that the hunter had hit the animal at the base of the horn and knocked it out momentarily. We tracked that deer for two hours and never found a drop of blood or a bit of hair, so it sure got away from us.

Another time my brother's hunter wounded a deer, and it went down into some brush and disappeared. By the time we got over there and eased up on it, a cougar had finished it off and was sitting there enjoying the meal.

Nick Frederick: I've got a story I call the Wedding Ring Buck. There is an old saying that the ring comes before the wedding. Well, the ring also comes before the buck.

It was the first week of November when we decided how we were going to push this good mule deer buck out to a hunter from Mississippi. He had hunted with us many times before, and it was the last day of his three-day hunt. My brother and I set up a drive that we hoped would put the big buck right past the hunter, who was waiting on point. We had already seen the buck and decided he was a trophy. The area we were hunting

The "Wedding Ring Buck," which gross scored 214+. (Photo courtesy Nick Frederick)

was in the prairie region of Alberta, a mostly open area with a small three- to four-acre patch of buck brush that had held trophy bucks for us over the years.

We set up the drive, and without a hitch the hunter's .243 rang out, and a good, solid 170+ buck went down. We celebrated our success by the traditional means of shaking hands and going over the hunt and the shot two or three times, and then proceeded to take pictures. At that point it was my job to field dress the buck. We loaded the buck into the truck, and it seemed like just another day in paradise. I washed my hands near the gut pile and then proceeded to make the trip back to camp to show everyone our fine buck.

I was having breakfast on Sunday morning with my wife, Trish, back in Edmonton, when she noticed I wasn't wearing my wedding ring. I explained to her that I never wear my wedding ring while I go deer hunting because I might lose it, and that it should be in the jewelry holder in the bedroom. Well, it wasn't, and I began to worry—about our marriage, that is! Was it all over as quickly as it had begun? I was convinced that I had taken it off before the hunting season had begun. I searched high and low, everywhere I could think it might be. That hunt for the ring on Sunday turned up nothing.

By that evening I had returned to Battle River Lodge to greet the next week's batch of eager hunters, but I couldn't stop thinking about the missing wedding ring. I began the next hunt with a three-day scouting trip, and I explained to my next hunter the traumatic issue I was facing. I told him I wanted to stop by the kill site from last week to see if I could recover the ring and save my marriage. I was convinced that the ring wasn't there, though, because I was certain I hadn't had it on.

Unfortunately, since the time of the kill, it had snowed and left about a half-inch covering the ground, and the gut pile was completely cleaned up. We could still see my tire tracks, though, and I noticed the area where I had washed my hands with a jug of water. To my surprise, nestled in the snow and creating a perfect hole, was the ring! Obviously it had fallen off while I washed my hands. I grabbed it out of the snow, knowing my marriage was on firm ground again!

As I walked back toward the truck, which was only forty yards away, I recall saying to my hunter, "Well, let's go find you a buck."

I had hardly finished the sentence when I spotted some deer moving around in the brush about three hundred yards down the hill. I quickly put the spotting scope up, and there was a great buck, one of the most magnificent muley bucks I had seen in a long time. He looked to be about 30 inches wide, with massive antlers and very deep forks. We viewed him for about ten minutes and then left the area so as not to disturb him before the season reopened in a couple of days.

On opening day we were in the area about an hour before daylight, and it was only about an hour after daylight that we spotted the buck. My hunter made a perfect shot on probably the biggest deer he will ever take. It made the Boone and Crockett record book with a gross score of 214+ and netted 194. I told my wife I had my priorities in order, though. The ring came before the buck!

Ask the Mule Deer Guides

Mick Chapel: We were up in northern New Mexico tracking a really big buck, one that had tracks that sank way down in the ground and splayed out the way the big ones always do. He was starting to wander around, and there were tracks all over the place. I knew he was right there, and I kept telling the guys to be ready. I could see where he'd been eating brush and cedar berries, and where he'd been raking his horns.

Another guide and I had four hunters with us, so I stationed them on the high ground across from where I thought the buck might be. We moved along, and all of a sudden all hell broke loose as the hunters spotted the deer spooking away from me. They fired fourteen times and hit the deer, but it was lightly wounded and kept right on going. I followed that buck for the next two full days, and those guys fired at it twenty-three more times before they got it. And to tell you the truth, I think the other guide actually killed the animal!

I don't think those guys liked me very much, because I put that buck in front of those hunters five different times and they couldn't kill it! I guess I wasn't very nice to them at the time. The best we could figure I had followed that deer for about seventeen miles before we finally got it on the ground.

Eduardo Gomez Jr.: One time a hunter asked me to put my hand over his left eye because he couldn't see the animal through his riflescope. I think it was a case of buck fever.

David Lopez: I had one hunter who shot a huge desert mule deer that we were sure was dead. We were so happy we were dancing around and celebrating. In the meantime, the deer got up on its feet and simply left the area while we weren't looking! It took us seven more hours to finally track it down and kill it. I'm now much more cautious about premature celebrating.

What do you see as the most critical environmental/ management/public relations issues affecting the future of mule deer hunting?

Grant Adkisson: I've got to do a little soap-boxing on this one. As much as I love all God's animals, I'd say one of the

Any hunter would love to get this giant on the ground! (Photo courtesy Jess Rankin)

most critical issues today is hunting and population control of mountain lions. I've hunted in a place in California where we used to see tremendous herds of mule deer and black-tailed deer, and they've been wiped out by mountain lions. I was at that same place recently, and we couldn't find a single deer. Now the rancher is losing cattle to mountain lions. To me, it's a matter of stewardship, and we're entrusted with keeping animal populations in balance.

I've seen mule deer numbers affected more by mountain lions than any other factor. Coyotes take quite a few fawns, but it's the cougars that are taking so many adult deer, and they preferentially take mature bucks that any hunter would love to have. Big bucks are generally alone, so there aren't as many eyes watching for lions. I found a beautiful nontypical mule deer buck last week that had been killed by a lion. The old conventional

Alberta produces some of the world's best and biggest bucks. (Photo courtesy Nick Frederick)

wisdom was that a lion kills only one deer per week, but that isn't true anymore, either. We've seen evidence of lions killing two or more deer per week.

The problem is that there are so many birds, with even crows and magpies now being protected species in Colorado. When a lion makes a kill, the birds find it and leave droppings all over it. A lion likes fresh, undisturbed meat, so when it walks up for a second feeding and finds its kill a mess, it just goes and kills another deer instead of finishing the first. Multiply that times six thousand mountain lions in Colorado and more than that number in California, and you get an idea of the magnitude of the problem and how many deer we're feeding to the lions. Mountain lions are magnificent animals and I appreciate them as much as any other animal, but their numbers need studied, solid management for the good of other wildlife.

Jeff Chadd: We need to get a hold on management and pay attention to what's going on. I think Colorado's current program is the very best, if they'll just hold the line on the number of tags they're issuing. Some other states need to follow Colorado's example, pay attention to tag numbers in relation to population and sex ratio, and manage the animals well for everybody, resident and nonresident. They're trying to squeeze the nonresident out more and more, unfortunately. At least the Department of Wildlife is listening to us on issues like this, and that's a big plus.

Robb Wiley: I think there needs to be a focus on loss of habitat, particularly winter range. In our area, we've got encroachment of oil and gas interests that are starting to affect a lot of winter range where the mule deer migrate. The oil and gas industry is making incredible amounts of money, and I think they need to use some of it to preserve the great mule deer hunting we've got. Money needs to be put back on the ground for habitat restoration, such as controlled burns, for planting bitterbrush, killing old sagebrush stands, rejuvenating the grasslands, improving forage, controlling predators, and the like.

Elk numbers on the winter range definitely need to be controlled, because when elk and mule deer are competing directly the mule deer always lose. We also need to limit human impact, because of the increase in shed antler hunting, videographers, and the like, all of which put pressure on big bucks to the point that they often don't survive the winter. People must manage themselves so as not to harm the deer population on the winter range. Often if a big buck is found on the winter range, people find out about it and put so much pressure on the animal that it will drop twenty to thirty inches of antler measurement the next season because of the stress. Everybody who hears about such an animal wants to take videos and photos. We've tried to do some educating because it's going to take cooperation of all interests to protect these mule deer in winter.

Keith Atcheson: Loss of habitat, human encroachment, subdivisions, and too much hunting pressure on public and private lands can all affect the future of mule deer hunting. Mule deer are nowhere near as adaptable to such pressures as white-tailed deer, and most game departments know this. There has to be a limited amount of hunting in any given area in order for mule deer populations to thrive. While some doe mule deer hunting may be necessary in areas where there are simply too many deer, in general I am opposed to taking doe mule deer. I have seen too many mule deer does taken too many times in Montana.

One of the biggest mistakes our game department makes in western Montana is the issuing of antlerless mule deer licenses. Deer numbers in western Montana and in particular in southwest Montana are far lower than they used to be because of unlimited resident hunting pressure in addition to liberal hunting seasons that include the entire month of November. When you combine those factors with loss of habitat, it's no wonder deer hunting in Montana is nothing like it was thirty or forty years ago. Unfortunately, neither the game department nor the public wants to make any large changes or sacrifices to promote the health of the mule deer herd. That makes finding a big muley in Montana pretty difficult. For the most part, central and eastern Montana mule deer populations are in great condition.

Doug Gardner: I'm really prejudiced on this one. I'm a hunter and a guide, but I'm also a private landowner. I can talk only about what I know, so I can't talk about mule deer in the high mountains of Colorado or the desert Southwest. Here, it's respecting private property rights, whether you're a hunter who drew a license or a state game management professional. There needs to be a balance between quality and quantity, and I think we've got a pretty good balance in eastern Montana right now. Those of us who promote quality management and who lease big chunks of private land for ourselves or our clients would like our position to be respected. And we should respect those who are quantity oriented. We need both types of management in Montana. The key to good mule deer hunting in southeastern Montana is good ranchers who raise good cattle and good deer on their properties.

Fred Lamphere: I think that our mule deer numbers are increasing, and I want to give credit where credit is due, and that's essentially rancher education. These ranchers have played the most important role in getting our mule deer numbers back to where they are today. That's true at least in our part of the country. The game departments have done their part, too, and they need some of the credit, but habitat is provided mostly by the ranchers. Our mule deer are as strong as they've been in my lifetime.

Thomas Brunson: Human encroachment on winter range is a big problem in some areas. Around our small town it isn't such a problem because we have only six thousand people, and we're the largest town for 250 miles. Another issue is piñon-juniper encroachment, which is choking out a lot of the bitterbrush and other food plants needed by mule deer. This has come about because of long-term fire suppression. They've even tried doing controlled burns, but the ground underneath has no residual population of desirable plants to repopulate it, so it all comes back as cheatgrass, which mule deer won't eat.

Troy Justensen: Here in Utah it comes down to habitat management and predator control. The problem is mainly coyotes, because Utah manages its lion population well. We lose a tremendous number of fawns every year to coyotes, and I think it's our number one problem. Most people don't hunt coyotes anymore, with fur prices being so low. A lucrative fur market would certainly help our deer herd.

Jess Rankin: Habitat loss is a big issue, because it's a major factor when there's a decline in mule deer numbers. Politics is another issue, because here in New Mexico we're not killing nearly enough cougars. Every time we try to get the game and fish people to raise the cougar quota, all the bleeding hearts show up at the meeting and protest to the high heavens. They claim to be for animal rights, but they don't seem to care about anything but predators. It's amazing to me that if they want to triple the number of elk tags all of them sit back and twiddle their thumbs while that's being debated. I don't know what makes those guys tick, but they seem to like only furry critters that eat other critters. Coyotes are another huge problem because they get a lot of fawns. When fur prices were good, back in the 1970s, there were a lot more mule deer than there are now, and that's not an accident.

Bowen Dolhan: Loss of habitat is a big problem in southern Alberta, where development is encroaching on the best ranges. It isn't such a big problem up here so far. Management by the game and fish departments is a really important issue, and we've seen the benefits of limiting the number of bucks taken here in Alberta. The main public relations problem is the decline in the number of hunters, because for some reason the younger generation just isn't picking it up the way we did when we were young. Here there are also fewer and fewer people living out in the country, and that affects hunter recruitment. Probably most of my generation was born and raised out on the countryside, but that isn't the case today. People in cities just don't understand the hunting way of life, and when they ask me why I hunt, I just can't explain it in a way they can understand. When I was a kid it was a way of life, as was trapping. City people don't understand that.

Harry Leuenberger: Fire suppression has cost us more deer habitat than any other factor. The Forest Service is just great at putting out fires, but we need some of those overgrown areas to burn to regenerate good conditions for wildlife. There is a lot of fir and pine forest that timber companies won't harvest, and it just keeps growing and squeezing out the best deer habitat. Also, you've got to manage predators if you're going to have any kind of quality hunting.

Nick Frederick: Mule deer hunting will be around for a long time in Alberta. There has been some oil and gas development that has shifted deer movement slightly, but the deer seem to be very adaptive. I foresee that mule deer hunting in Alberta will be excellent for many years to come, as deer numbers have never been so high.

Mick Chapel: Money is a big positive factor in Mexico. It's affecting the deer herd in a very good way, because they now realize what a valuable resource they have. The cowboys can shoot all the javelina they want for the pot, but that rancher had better not catch them shooting deer. They're too valuable to be used for meat.

Eduardo Gomez Jr.: Our laws unfortunately allow people with no experience to begin an outfitting business here in Sonora. These people do not hesitate to take young animals, and they are not doing anything to help the habitat or the mule deer. That is

Sonora produces some of the world's greatest mule deer bucks. (Photo courtesy Eduardo Gomez)

causing the mule deer to be overhunted badly in some areas of Sonora. It isn't a problem everywhere, but it has the potential to harm mule deer hunting here in the near future.

David Lopez: In many areas of Sonora too many licenses are issued for too small an area. That will eventually come back to haunt both us and the hunters who book such places.

Do you have any parting words of wisdom for mule deer hunters?

Grant Adkisson: Do your homework, get to know your equipment, and practice all you can.

Jeff Chadd: I'd say you've just got to be patient to get a trophy mule deer.

Robb Wiley: Take advantage of your luck. There's an old football definition of luck as being when patience, preparation, and persistence meet. So do your homework and take advantage of it when your chance comes.

Keith Atcheson: My advice to mule deer hunters is this: If you and your party are interested in a good hunt for an average,

Hunting mule deer requires a lot of patience and a lot of glassing.

representative animal, then hunting in Wyoming and Montana, in the central and eastern ends of each state, offers great hunting, high success, fairly easy terrain, and a lot of fun. For hunters looking for above-average to exceptional mule deer, go where they have been consistently produced historically. In my opinion, the best current areas for big deer are Utah, Arizona, Nevada, and, of course, my favorite, Mexico. Seek out the best outfitter or guide you can afford, or do all your homework if you decide to go it on your own. Most Western states have great mule deer hunting, but it's difficult to obtain a tag in most of the best areas. If you want to be sure you get to go hunting, plan on an area where you will be guaranteed a license. Otherwise, put your name in the hat and see what happens. Be persistent in the drawings. Don't expect to draw anything, and be pleasantly surprised if you do.

Doug Gardner: Come mule deer hunting fully prepared mentally. Know that the higher a standard you set for yourself, the more difficult the chore becomes and the lower the chances of success. Hunters need to be ready to endure the extra effort it takes and to take advantage of even a split-second opportunity when it presents. A trophy mule deer may very well be the hardest trophy to take in North America. My personal definition of a trophy, though, is a deer with a hunter behind it wearing a big smile!

Fred Lamphere: I can't stress good optics enough, plus really spending the time to study where you'll be hunting. That's your catch-and-release on mule deer, and what allows you to know what's there.

Thomas Brunson: Get in shape and make sure you can shoot! For mule deer hunters who are on their own, get the best optics you can and get out and use them well before the season starts.

Troy Justensen: When you're hunting, never give up! There's a bright future because a lot of good organizations have risen to the task of helping mule deer. I believe we'll see a remarkable recovery of mule deer numbers in most states in the future.

Jess Rankin: First, if you want to kill a big mule deer, you have to hunt where there are big mule deer. Next, you've got to learn how to hit a moving target.

Bowen Dolhan: The biggest challenge we've had over the years has been to teach hunters that ground hunting by spot and stalk is very different from tree stand hunting. We have lots of hunters who have killed plenty of game from tree stands; they come up here and find that things are totally different. It's another learning curve, and unless they realize that ahead of time and are prepared for it, the hunt may be over before they start to tune in. Another point is not to give up until the hunt is over. We take just as many deer on the last day of a hunt as we do on the first day. When a hunter takes a deer at the very last moment, it's always because he never gave up. Those guys who give up mentally, or who go home early, will never have that last-minute triumph.

Harry Leuenberger: Get in shape, and then go hunting and have fun. That's what it's all about. A lot of people are much too serious about wanting to kill an animal, but that's actually just a bonus. Being out there in fantastic, beautiful country and seeing the scenery and the animals—that's the real payoff.

Nick Frederick: Mule deer are a beautiful trophy and have become one of my major passions. If you have not taken a great mule deer, you should look upon it as a challenge to take a good buck, because it's very satisfying when you do. I am sure you will get the mule deer bug and attempt to fill a wall with bucks after your first successful hunt.

Mick Chapel: Get on it now, man, because mule deer hunting is now in the "good old days." The way the state of New Mexico is managing, or rather not managing, its mule deer herd, there isn't going to be any mule deer hunting on public land here within a few years. I could go on and on about the reasons why, but that's the simple truth.

Eduardo Gomez Jr.: Keep supporting the hunting of this magnificent animal by first of all taking care of the mule deer and doing the hunt in the right way. That will mean more and bigger animals over the years.

David Lopez: The hunter must never give up. He should start out each day with a huge supply of patience and always keep trying. He should remember that the more difficult the hunt, the more he will appreciate the fine trophy he takes as a result of his effort and perseverance.